RU NEW?

"A New Way of Life"

MJ Broussard

TESTIMONIALS

TEXT CONVERSATION WITH JW.

"Good evening, Mike. This is JW. We met this afternoon for the (in my opinion) most rewarding orientation I've ever completed. I just wanted to thank you for sharing your time and wisdom to help a little girl you have never met. My wife and I really appreciate your help!! P. S - We can't wait for the book to come out, so good luck finishing the masterpiece."

"I feel blessed to be given an opportunity to help others. A locket or medallion with RU NEW? inscribed. Who knows, if all three of you use The RU NEW Principles, it may triple the outcome!"

"I like it, and we are all behind it, sir!!"

TEXT CONVERSATION WITH D. ROUGEAU

"RU New?"

"Roger that brother. Are you new? Same level or higher? Brother, I am doing amazing. I had some good conversations at home Sunday night, then the good and bad news this week, but keeping that charge forward with a new mindset. You have no idea how much that statement means to me. I'm blessed to have met you."

"I am so thankful that I could have a positive impact. It is a great and awesome principle and a way of life!"

"I'm a firm believer everyone comes into contact for a reason. To be honest, I was at the bottom of the barrel and struggling with my inner demons and life in general. After meeting you and having that conversation, I constantly ask people who talk to me (I have quite a few people I know unload on me) that simple question you taught me. Are you New? And we go into it, and I'm literally taking things in such a better stride. You're stuck with me forever, lol. I refer to you as my mentor."

"And you will be one of the first I give a copy of my book."

"It helped to push out the comfort zones. That has helped make my relationship with my family easier. It brings me to that higher level, "New me," daily. It's little victories for me and little victories for them because it's allowing us to do more as a family. My wife and I are at an all-time high in our relationship right now compared to where it has been the last couple of years. So, all this rambling comes down to this: I am thankful for the day you spent with me and just talking. You've helped open my mind in a way I've never thought. It's helped me be able to start making changes in myself to be a better person. It's helping me strengthen my relationships and give more trust, time, and respect to the people in my life. You never know who you run into and how they will impact your life."

Table of Contents

INTRODUCTION

This thought, this state of mind, this idea came to me several years ago. I have studied and utilized these principles to better my life and share with others during this time. Because I have shared these principles with others who were in need with tremendous results, I was encouraged to put them into book form.

Though it has been a struggle to learn what writing method to use, it has been realized that it had to be written just as the principals teach, New. I was inspired by my wife, Lois. Christmas of 2021, she gave me a journal with a writing pen. On the pen was inscribed "Am I New?" My focus was on this book and those people in need. I lost sight of the real reason for writing this book. The question must be asked of myself first, and the answer must come from me. That said, from that day forward until

February 2, 2022, I worked on myself and my method of sharing *"The RU NEW Principles"*.

Although transformative and life-changing, the principles cannot be shared unless one truly has made it the focus of one's life. Don't get me wrong, the focus of my life will always be my family. But, to be the best husband, father, and friend, I must first focus on myself. I must become the best me that I can possibly be. So, although the statement is very broad, it will always begin with the first step. So, the first step is to ensure that the principles I'm about to share with you have been practiced and believed by the one sharing them.

I can truly say that these principles have made me a better man, a better husband, a better father, and a better friend.

So the first step we will take is also the title of this book.

Asking yourself, Are you New? So let's dig into the question itself.

We live our lives according to the outcome of our day's past. We allow the past to determine this moment in life. We are driven to judge the next step using what we cannot change. The path we have taken cannot be undone. But the attitude you decide upon will determine the journey before you. Allowing yourself to judge today strictly by yesterday will eventually lead you back to the same worn path and destination.

So, you must ask yourself, do I want to change my path? If you are like most, your answer is a variety of answers. Can you ignore the outcome of your journey called life? Absolutely not! Should you forget the lessons you have learned? The emotions that you have felt? The wisdom you have gained? Never! This is who you are!

So, where does that leave us? Is the path already set? How do we change the outcome of today and the future? No matter your answer to the question, how has my life turned out so far? You can determine the outcome of today and your tomorrow. Up to this point, you have based your vision of today and your outlook of tomorrow strictly on previous victories and failures. And this has always determined your future.

But you can change the path before you. How is this accomplished? How do you determine the outcome? How do you change the path once traveled? A path that has led you to this destination? How do you change your future, even if you continue down the same path?

The answer always has been and always will be ATTITUDE. Your attitude has brought you to this moment in your life. No matter the outcome, your attitude has and always will determine your results.

While there are many tremendous self-help books and seminars at your access that are beneficial and can be life-changing, there are none that focus on that one question that will change your attitude and your life! This simple question can change every aspect of your life. It can determine the path, the outcome, and your future!

The question is:

ARE YOU NEW?

PART ONE

THE AWAKENING

LEARNING TO BE NEW

CHAPTER 1

THE HUMBLE ABODE
HOME LIFE

Let's begin with the first step of this journey; The moment your eyes open to begin your day is when you set the foundation with your attitude for the rest of this day and all the days to come.

If you are like me, you begin to focus the moment your eyes open. You ask yourself questions. How did I sleep? How do I feel? Am I hungry? What do I want to eat? I can't wait for a cup of coffee! Some people will answer these questions and take care of the tasks before contemplating how this day will begin and end. For others, the journey before them is one of the first thoughts that cross their mind. Then, your mind will drift to yesterday. Finally, you will evaluate and determine this day based on the outcome of yesterday.

This can be very pleasurable, or it can be very disturbing. You will view your day with optimism and joy, or it will be a vision of pessimism and dread. Both are your choice. Both are an attitude. You determine your attitude. But that is easier said than done. If you are like most, you will allow yesterday to control today. You will allow the outcome of yesterday to determine the attitude for today. You have set your attitude in stone, and there is very little that will change this attitude. This is what we normally do. But it's time to change that!

It is time to begin our day with an attitude that will bring joy to your heart and enhance your life. Your attitude will allow you to determine the outcome of today and the rest of your life.

RU NEW?

Today is a *New* day. No matter what happened yesterday, there is absolutely nothing that you can do that will change that. The only thing that you can change is the next thought, feeling, and attitude. This will determine the outcome of your day, no matter the hurdles that are placed before you.

You must set your foundation for today. You must begin your journey on the right path. You must have the right attitude. You cannot change what has happened. But you can change your attitude no matter what life has in store for you.

But you say that this is easier said than done. I agree to a certain extent. We have created habits that are locked into the fibers of our souls. You begin your day the same way every day. You have created habits that have determined your outcome. How do you change your habits? How do you change your outcomes? Well, if you want to make changes in your life, then you must make changes in your life. You must change your habitual nature. You have been determining your future based on your past.

You must change your routine. You wake up and have a cup of coffee. You make ready your breakfast. You contemplate your day. Then, based on your habits, you determine your attitude for today. I am sure that the steps may be different for everyone. But the one absolute step is determining your attitude. You need help. You need a guide. You need *The RU NEW Principles* to change your attitude and outlook for today. It comes down to one question. Are You New?

So, let's set the foundation. The cornerstone of these principles begins at the waking hour. You must change your habits when your eyes open. You must set your foundation for the day. What is very helpful is to place little reminders in unavoidable spots. Like most, we use an alarm clock to wake. Putting something near the alarm that is a trigger point is very helpful. Use a card, a sticky note, or an object which will be your trigger point. It will focus on your thought process. You are trying to create a New habit to replace your old habits. On the trigger point, you may want to write "Are You New?" Or anything else that is a trigger for you. Whether it be a sticky note, an object, or anything else, it needs to be something that focuses you on changing your focus for the morning. Allow yourself some time to utilize this trigger point. Allow time to transform your first thoughts when you wake.

Normally, when you wake, your first thoughts are focused on your daily tasks. Then we contemplate our yesterday. No matter the morning's condition or yesterday's outcome, you are striving to change your viewpoint. And the only way that will change is if you change the processes and the attitudes you habitually use.

RU NEW?

No matter your situation, you have control of your future. But you have to make the first step. So that little sticky note or whatever it is that you use is that first step. Now, how do we use that?

The alarm goes off. You turn the light on. You rub your eyes; you stretch, and then you focus. Then there it is that sticky note. On that sticky note, it says *RU NEW?* The goal is to transform your mind immediately. Are You New? Well, are you? This becomes a filter. It's designed to filter out the habits that have created struggle and strife in your life. If you ask yourself this question immediately upon waking, you will begin transforming your first steps of the day. This is the first day! Be excited! These are the first steps to transforming your life into what you have always wanted it to be! Focus! Transform! Change!

So, there you go! You've taken the first step! Now, you ask, why am I doing this? You may begin to fall back into the habits of yesterday. You may tell yourself that this will never work. You may convince yourself that your life cannot be improved. Your situation will never change. This is where you have been. That is the old you. Where you are at this moment, whether it be good or bad, can always be better. Do you want today to be better than yesterday? Do you want your life to change in a positive direction? If your answer is no, I encourage you to continue reading. No matter how bad your situation is at the moment, deep down inside, we all strive to have better days.

You are now transforming your focus. You're changing your habits and mindset. This is the first day! You are transforming your mind, body, and soul. These are the steps to a Better Way of Life! So, quit doubting yourself. You, and only you, have control of your attitude. Every one of us has the ability to control our attitude. But you need to learn how to focus on the task at hand. Like most, we struggle to change our habits. The root cause of the roadblocks to change is doubt.

You are awake. You have found your trigger. You have asked yourself, "RU New?" Then there it is. You have exclaimed, "I AM NEW!" For some, that little tinge of doubt may set in. It's human nature. But now it's time to take action! It's time to change your habits. It's time to eliminate doubt. If you allow doubt to control your journey, you'll likely end up right back at the same destination. If you are experiencing doubt, then it is absolutely necessary for you to focus on *The RU NEW Principles*. First, you must ask yourself once again, "Am I New?" Then, continue asking yourself the same question until the answer is absolutely "YES! I AM NEW!!". Once you have overcome any doubt, you are ready to apply *The RU NEW Principles* to your daily life.

You've taken your shower. You've gotten dressed, and now you're ready to enter the world with your New Attitude. You open the bedroom door and walk down the hall into the kitchen. And there it is! The chaos of day-to-day life hits you right between the eyes. The kids are arguing. The dogs are begging for treats. Your significant other is not too optimistic about their day. Maybe a stack of bills was left on the kitchen table from last night. Maybe a sink full of dirty dishes. Regardless of what it is, there are thousands of triggers that will pull you back into the habits of yesterday. But you are in control. No matter what you think, it is up to you to determine your attitude as this day begins. Unfortunately, we all have the tendency to let what happened yesterday, or what was left in the kitchen, determine how we approach today.

RU NEW?

At the moment, you cannot change what is in front of you. But you can ask yourself if You Are New. In the past, the way you handled the morning chaos may have created a level of anxiety that determined the rest of your day. Either you can allow it to control you, or you can focus, ask yourself, "RU NEW?" and determine a better path for today! Each day you meet the morning chaos with a new attitude, and you will find that the chaos will begin to be less controlling. Why? Those around you will see and feel the difference in your New attitude. It will begin to transform them as well. You will find that the chaos will begin to decrease. If it doesn't decrease, you will become better at handling the morning turmoil. You cannot let those around you control your attitude. It is up to you to be in control. And you can definitely control your attitude by implementing The RU NEW Principles and asking yourself, "RU NEW?"

RU NEW?

This method will work for you, no matter what your situation is. Why? When you are New, or should we say, when your attitude is New, your perspective of the situation becomes one of learning. What is meant by learning? Under normal circumstances, we have programmed thinking. When you ask yourself *RU NEW* and reply Yes, your mind frame and demeanor transform into a learning mode. When you live controlled by yesterday, you base your decisions on things in the past. We create habits that we become comfortable with. Sometimes, comfortable can become very uncomfortable. Programming oneself to be comfortable with excepting an outcome or situation without allowing yourself the opportunity to grow can be very uncomfortable.

You must believe your answer when you ask yourself, "*RU NEW?*" "I Am *NEW!*" This may be immediate, or it may take some time.

RU NEW?

Regardless, you are developing a way of life that allows you to look at all situations as a New Experience. A life that you have control of. What is meant by control of? You have control of your viewpoint and attitude. When you are New, you become open-minded to whatever situation you will face. Do you remember things that you have done for the first time? Do you remember how energetic you were about learning that skill? You were New! You were more receptive to learning than you will ever be. You know beyond a shadow of a doubt that you must learn a new skill to become proficient at the task. As time passed, you became more knowledgeable and hopefully proficient at the task. Then, human nature kicks in, and you begin to form habits. The habits that you developed allow you to progress forward. But in most cases, those same habits will begin to close your mind to learning and never to learn at that level again. So, by asking yourself, "*RU NEW?*" every single day and maybe every moment depending on the situation, you will program yourself for maximum learning every single day. You must believe that "*UR NEW!*". You must believe that any situation is an opportunity to learn. When you Master the skill, you will then truly be New! When you are New, you will not allow the habits of your yesterdays to dictate your actions and attitudes of today. You must remain New.

Let's continue down the transformative and exciting path of being New! Let's take the huge leap into the concrete world!

"UR NEW!"

CHAPTER 2

THE JUNGLE

VENTURING OUT

Now you've taken the right steps at home. You're beginning to change your attitude towards the chaos within your humble abode. You're feeling better about yourself. Your stress levels have decreased. Your mind is right. You're beginning to believe that You Are New. You have a smile on your face and joy in your heart. Now it's time for the true test.

It's time to venture out into the world outside your domain. You know, as well as I that the true test is to come. Your home may be blissful, or it may be a full-blown war zone. Regardless, it pales compared to the trials and stress of the outside world. But you cannot be a hermit and live your whole life within your home.

Therefore, you need to arm yourself with your New Weapon that will allow you to handle any situation thrown your way. So grab your keys, wallet or purse, and your travel mug of coffee. Let's walk out into the world.

You get to your car, and it's a wonderful dreary rainy day. You forget your keys. You forget your wallet or purse or whatever it is that you forgot. The old mind frame is triggered once again. The car won't start, or the car is running rough. When you back out of the driveway, you almost hit a passing vehicle. You run over the garbage can or back into the neighbor's parked car. All of the morning issues are piling up. Or it may be just one simple incident. Regardless of the situation, you must ask yourself, "Will I continue being stressed every day by inevitable events?". Or will you practice being New? As soon as the feelings of stress, anger, anxiety, or any negative feelings begin to take over, you must stop your mind for just a moment. Look at yourself in the mirror and ask, "*RU NEW?*". Well, Are You New?

This is a work in progress, people. I know firsthand we have lived our entire life reacting to situations with a programmed mindset. You may be that person that allows every little thing to annoy you. Or that person that internalizes all of the stresses of life. But the reality is we are all under a certain level of stress. How we handle the stress determines our path forward. We can allow the stress to dictate a miserable day. Or we can use these moments to grow and become that Stronger New Person. First, you must take a breath and ask the question. Then, you must learn from the moment. You must be thankful that you were given a stressful situation that allows you to grow as a person. Eventually, you will look at these moments as a positive influence in your life. You Are New! Your typical reaction is the past. You have a choice.

You are on the road in the morning traffic with all the chaos. The old-minded lackadaisical stressed-out drivers are driving you insane. The person that's tailgating you, honking their horn, and shouting profanities at you. One that speeds by you cuts you off and then slows down. Some do not understand what a turn signal is. The people were swerving in their lane as if they were still drunk from the night before. The whole world seems to be out to get you. People, this is our normal morning commute. The commute sets the tone for the rest of the day, along with the chaos at home. You may not be a city dweller. You may have to deal with snow and ice in a mountain pass. You may have to deal with washed-out roads. You may have to deal with the worst roads on earth. There will be hazardous conditions and crazy drivers every day. But, regardless of the conditions, the scenario is pretty much the same. The stress is beginning to build. Your attitude is beginning to go down the tubes. Here is one of those moments. Thank goodness you have a newfound weapon that will allow you to deal with the craziness of the demolition derby that we call our commute.

Do you have a bad case of road rage? Are you a grumbler? Are you that person that internalizes everything? Regardless of who you are, times like these create negative habits. Those negative habits will determine your attitude for today and eventually tomorrow. Put a smile on your face and joy in your heart because you are a New Person! You have a new attitude! You get to a boiling point, and you ask the question. You know the question and the answer. You can't allow the habits of yesterday to completely eliminate the progress that you have made today.

RU NEW?

You can scream and holler at the car on the side of you. It may feel good at the moment, but it does nothing good for your attitude. But, you can control the stress and anger. *UR NEW!* You need to realize this and begin believing. What is important? Is it to get to work on time? Is it to get there in one piece? Will this be the same every day? Can you avoid this situation?

Until now, the commute has been a source of stress and anxiety. But today, *UR NEW!* Today you will grow as a person! Today you have ammunition that you didn't have yesterday. You must ask yourself, "Do I want to be New?". If the answer is yes, then you must begin growing as a person and a defensive driver, of course. Maybe it's the route that you take. Maybe it's the speed that you drive. There are many factors involved when trying to get from point A to point B. Regardless; you are still met with the stresses of commuting.

RU NEW?

UR NEW! You have looked yourself in the eye. Have you decided that stress will no longer control you? You will grow as a person. And maybe become a better driver, Ha, ha, ha! But ultimately, you control the situation and your attitude. You must calm down and take a deep breath. You must decide that you control your world. The world does not control you. This is the foundation of *The RU NEW Principles*.

Oh, thank goodness! You made it! You're in the driveway of your job or business. Your blood pressure is elevated, and your stress level has increased. But, because of your newfound weapon called *The RU NEW Principles*, you have handled the turmoil better today than you did yesterday.

You found a parking spot and turned the car off. The next reality check surfaces. It is your next test. Whether you despise or thoroughly enjoy your means of income, it will have challenges and triggers. For some, their source of income can be their greatest stress. There are many forms of stress involved. For others, it is a way of life. It may be the priority of their life. Regardless of whether you work to live or you live to work, you will definitely have turmoil. The turmoil that will revert you back to the habits of yesterday. In the past, it has slightly or completely controlled you. But those days are over!

It is time to take a stand! Before you open that door, stop. Self-check time. Take a deep breath. Ask yourself, *RU NEW?* Don't just go through the motions. Stare deep into your soul and believe the answer. "I Am New!"

What controlled you yesterday will no longer control you today. You are going to walk in with a newfound attitude. You have a weapon. You are becoming New. Take another deep breath, smile, and be overjoyed. This day will be an opportunity for you to grow as a person. It is an opportunity to become better at whatever it is that you do to earn an income. You have to be NEW!

Do you remember the first day at a new job? Do you remember your excitement? Do you remember how you were a sponge? You learned so much, and you absorbed a whole new optimistic atmosphere. In most instances, you learned more in the beginning than you are learning today. You were excited about the new opportunity. You were overwhelmed with optimism for your newfound source of income. In some situations, you were happy to just have a source of income. Regardless, you were New. You were walking down the path of *The RU NEW Principles*. Without understanding its impact on your life, you were functioning at a Higher Level of New. So, before you exit your vehicle, rekindle that excitement. Become New again. Become receptive to learning. Understand and accept the hurdles that will be placed in your path today. Be excited about it. It is an opportunity to grow and learn.

Onward! Reality kicks in. Whether it was last night, this morning, or when you walk through the door, the struggles of yesterday will surface. But You Are New! Did you decide to learn from the struggles of yesterday? Or did you decide to allow yesterday dictate an attitude of dread and despair? It's your decision. It's easy to wallow in the negativity of yesterday. And the prospect of the negativity being compounded today is probable.

You have to ask yourself the question, "RU NEW?". Does it sound redundant? In the beginning, it will. But you are developing newfound energy. You are developing a mindset. You're creating a habit that will change your life! So, you must ask the question. And depending on how many stressful events you have in your life, you may have the need to ask the question very often. As you grow and get stronger, the need to ask yourself the question becomes less. Why is that? Because you are seeing the glorious benefit of the New You. You are believing the answer "I Am New!" You will begin to subconsciously ask yourself the question, give yourself the answer and begin to believe it deep down in your soul. You are becoming the New You! And you will definitely reap the rewards!

Here you go. You are now entering the realm of gainful employment. There may be a supervisor. Or it might be the owner. How about coworkers? There may be people working for you. In all instances, you are dealing with people. People who are not new. People that do not have your attitude, your drive, or desire. They can be an enormous supply of stress and a contributing factor to the potential for anxiety.

But now, it doesn't matter because you are in control. And as you become better at being New, you will begin to see a positive change. Positive energy in all aspects of your life, including your job or business. Why?

One of your coworkers is complaining about the boss. The boss is complaining about one of your coworkers. The boss and coworkers are complaining to each other. It may be your supervisor has unrealistic goals or demands. You are surrounded by negativity. Do not focus on the negative energy these people are radiating. It is vitally important for you to focus all of your energy on yourself. You are growing into the New You. Yes, you must listen. And in some instances, you will have to take action. But, in the past, you have allowed negativity and unrealistic goals to dictate your attitude. Your attitude dictated your stress level. And your stress level dictates your quality of life.

RU NEW?

People! I am telling you that *The RU New Principals* will transform your life! It will positively transform your relationships at work and all other realms of your life. Do not let them drag you down. Do not drag yourself down. It is time to take a stand! Once again, you must ask yourself, "Am I in Control? Am I New? Yes, I Am!" And you are beginning to believe it deep down in your soul.

Now, you ask the question. How would this change anything at my job or my business? Well, let's look at it simply. You walked into that domain this morning with a New Attitude. Whether or not your coworkers or supervisor are personally working on themselves, your Newfound attitude and energy will be infectious. You will begin to feel the stress becoming less and less. You will begin to smile more. You will feel better. And don't think that this will go unnoticed. Your energy and excitement will be radiated. This will create a positive wave among all the people associated with you. If you are the supervisor, the same applies to you. You are New! You have a New Attitude. Your energy levels are climbing, and it's very evident to the people around you. Your coworkers will be curious. Some will be jealous, but jealous in a good way. They will see the New You. The pessimistic will say, The New You is a brief moment that will pass. But as you master your craft of being New, your coworkers will not only begin to believe; they will become curious and ask questions.

Everyone in your life will be curious. As time goes on, they will be envious. Regardless if they decide to become a New person, your Newness will become a positive influence in their life. Their energies will change. Your boss's energy will change. The energy of the people working for you will change. In other words, you are in control! This is very powerful!

You have the power to learn. You have the power to influence. You have the power to change other people's lives. But first, you have to change yours. You have to become New. From this point forward, you will be in complete control.

This New found energy, this New You, will allow you to learn and grow as you did when you first started your job or business. You are receptive. You are not allowing past stresses to dictate your ability to grow as a person and worker. By becoming New, you have become a sponge. With your New Attitude, you will begin learning and growing at a higher level. You will stop being a participant in the negative atmosphere. Your confidence levels will begin to rise. You begin to grow daily. And this will make you more valuable each and every day.

RU NEW?

You will take pleasure in the New You. You will be pleased that you have become a better worker or business owner. You Are New!

Exponential! This will begin to compound. Your energy and attitude will begin affecting those around you. You will feel your stress and anxiety begin to subside. They will appreciate you. You will appreciate You. And as you grow, so will they. They will grow without even knowing it. You will be instrumental in their transformation. Your supervisor, your coworkers, and your business associates will all benefit from the New You. Now, do you understand how *The RU NEW Principles* will transform your life? Do you understand that you are in control? Do you believe that You Are New? Do you believe that you can be New? As your journey continues, the answers to all those questions become obvious. Yes, I Am New!

RU NEW?

Does it result in profit margins rising? Does it transition into a raise or a promotion? Do you become more optimistic about your job or business? Regardless of your question, the most important question to ask yourself is *RU NEW?*

Every day you show up for work, your levels of Newness will have grown. The amount of influence that you have on yourself and those around you will begin to grow. In time, the effects become evident. You are learning more. You are becoming a better supervisor, employee, or business owner. You are becoming a better friend. People around you become more and more curious. And your positive effect on them will begin to reduce your stress and anxiety. Without it being said, it will have an enormous positive impact on your life.

But there are those people. Individuals that will journey down the path of life in nothing but misery and despair. Their true source of enjoyment and justification is to make your life miserable. They do not want to be miserable alone. They take joy in your despair. Their goal is to make you as miserable as they are. Do you know people like this? Do you understand these people exist? Do you understand how much of a positive influence they can be in your life? And now you ask the question, what in the world are you talking about? Well, let's talk about this.

Until this moment, that individual has created stress and anxiety in your life. You showed up to work in the morning, dreading the encounter with this person. You left in the evening angry at the fact that you will have to be exposed to this person tomorrow. You have brought that home to your family and loved ones. Heck, you've brought it home to your dog. They feel your stress as well. You think about that person. You talk about them. You complain about them. They become a huge focal point in your life.

Plainly said, they are steering your attitude. Up until now, you may feel like you are in control. But realistically, they are controlling you. They are controlling your attitude. And that is the plain truth! It may not be your boss. It may be a coworker. It does not matter who it is. Are you going to allow them to control you? Are you going to allow them to dictate who you are? Or will you use them to grow?

Do you understand that they can be a positive influence on your life? Do you understand how wide the gates of learning will open because of them? Unfortunately, some of the greatest influences in our life will come from the most negative situations or individuals.

So, as you grow into the New You, you will look at this person and smile! Understand that this person will be instrumental in your positive steps toward becoming the New You. They will be responsible for you becoming a better person, a better friend, and an all-around Better You. Each day you encounter this person, your attitude becomes progressively more positive. As time goes by, they will be responsible for transforming your focus. The transformation goes from focusing on the despair caused by this person to focusing on your positive transformation. They have put you in this frame of mind. Now you view this person as a positive influence. You begin seeing the positive outcome from the negative situation. Then your focus migrates back to you. Your focus is one on Newness. It's a focus on positive change. It is a focus on learning. It is a focus of a New You!

Now you are beginning to understand that you are in control. But also realizing that you have limited control over the people around you, and as you grow as a New Person, your influence will grow stronger. What a negative person was in your life has transformed into an asset in your growth. It is as simple as making a decision. Using *The RU NEW Principles*, you now have the ability to not only change who you are, but that ability reaches out to others as well. Who knows? This individual may transform into a new person like you. If they do not, you will always be thankful for the positive influence their negative life has bestowed on you.

So, you gather your stuff. It is the end of the day. Today may have been a struggle. But remember, it was a needed struggle. Before you walk out that door, you must pause for a second. You must look at your surroundings with a smile on your face. You must ask yourself, "Did I achieve a Higher Level of New today?" Am I a Newer Person? Did my Newness positively influence anyone's world today? What did I learn? Am I better prepared for tomorrow's workday than I was when I walked in this morning? And, how much more do I believe that I Am New?

You are preparing yourself for tomorrow's work world adventure. You are also preparing yourself for the journey across the asphalt jungle. But unlike this morning, you are a Newer Person. Your Newness has a little bit more time and experience to lean on. You are better prepared.

We have touched on a couple of aspects of your life so far. They have been a source of stress, anxiety, and despair. In your mind, you may say that your job and your household have never been a source of stress. But I asked the question, has it ever been a source? Or do you deny the pieces of this puzzle? There is a constant struggle between positive and negative in every aspect of our lives. We may not see the struggle. But I tell you, it is there. So, what is good in your mind, will only get better. When it comes to your life,

RU NEW?

you may want to ask, "Am I a Better New Person?

The benefits of *The RU NEW Principles* are there for everyone, no matter the amount of struggle they are in. Using these Principles will correct and enhance all aspects of your life.

The lunatics of the daily commute will still be there. Upon arriving at your home, you may realize that the chaotic atmosphere is still there. The bills are still there. What you left this morning may still be there. But the difference is that you have grown as a New Person today. You have a better outlook. You have a more fine-tuned approach to dealing with the chaos. And overtime, you begin to control the levels of chaos. Or, because of your positive influence on those around you, they may begin to decrease their contribution to the chaos. Regardless, you are in control. You Are New!

RU NEW?

You have made it home. Hopefully safe and sound. Of course, there were other challenges during your travels. It may have been the normal day-to-day hurdles of navigation. It may have been very eventful. Hopefully not. But you overcame and conquered. Pause for just a second. Be excited about the New Person you are becoming. Be thankful for the challenges of the day because they are merely an opportunity for growth. You may be excited about your day being chaotic and stressful. But what you should be more excited about is that you met those challenges, utilized *The RU NEW Principles*, and have grown into a New and Better Person.

Now, you head into the house. The reason for growth meets you at the door. Instead of hello, how was your day? You may be hit with all of their challenges of the day. The dogs are barking. The kids are arguing. The house is a mess. Food needs to be cooked. And nobody can decide what they would like to eat. It is just one more welcomed hurdle. Be excited! You have grown. You are the New You. Today, your domestic challenges are less stressful than yesterday's. Meet them with a smile on your face, joy in your heart, and the glow of your Newness.

You may be staying at home tonight, or you may be going out to dinner. Maybe a night on the town regardless of what your plans are, there will be challenges. Menu issues. Destination challenges. Logistic issues. What to wear or where to go. The old you would allow this to be a source of anxiety. But you must continue practicing your craft. No matter the issue, you must ask yourself if You Are New. And believe that you are. Once you have established that, your decisions will become far less stressful.

Along the way, you will encounter people that will attempt to trick you and make you stumble. It does not matter if it is intentional or if they are just individuals who live their lives as old people. You are not claiming to be a better person. You are a New Person that is growing with every encounter. Your attitude and energy will be instrumental in transforming others into less confrontational people. Why? Because you are becoming less confrontational. You are a New Person. There is absolutely no reason to allow individuals to control your attitude or path. It's up to you. You are in control. Believe in the principles and believe in yourself. Take time to Marvel in your growth. The positive affirmation will be infectious. What caused you despair has become an opportunity to better yourself and those around you.

As you grow, you will find that you will be less involved in chaotic encounters. Why? It is your New Energy. The positive energy within you will radiate. And as you grow into a New

RU NEW?

Person, most people you encounter will benefit from it. Positive energy attracts positive energy.

One wants mac & cheese. The other wants pizza. Your significant other has had a terrible day and has decided that you should participate in their negative outlook. The dog can't make up its mind if it's hungry or it wants to go outside. The dishes are piling up. The house needs to be swept and mopped. The dishwasher quit working. No one will take the garbage out. Yes, it is the normal evening.

Under the previous circumstances, or should I say yesterday, you would allow this chaos to dictate your attitude. You would get caught up in the moment and allow the chaos to be your source of anxiety. But, today, You Are New! You have a new outlook on the turmoil of your dwelling. So, you must take a breath and ask yourself if You Are New. Do you have a different approach? Do you have a New view?

RU NEW?

Are you better prepared to handle the chaos? You must allow yourself to grow during every moment of your life. That includes kids screaming, dogs barking, and all of the evening chaos.

I know. Everyone's situation is different. You are saying that the chaos of family life does not apply to you. Yes, family life may not be applicable. But the chaos is. The empty dwelling still has its chaos. You know this to be true. It may be less of an opportunity for growth. And in your mind, it may be a beneficial thing. Don't get me wrong; I wish for lack of chaos for all people. But that is not realistic. You still have struggles regardless of whether it involves people or pets in your home. You may eat out every evening. There is chaos and stress there. You may live a quiet life. But life is still there. There are challenges around every corner. Some are external, and others are internal. We all have struggles. *The RU NEW Principles* will benefit anyone that is willing to utilize them.

The evening has ended. Or if you work nights, the night has ended. You may be that individual that never sleeps. Regardless, there comes a time when we all have to physically and mentally shut down to recharge our batteries and soul. A key component of being New is to analyze what you have learned. Recall the moments of growth today. You must see the growth. You must marvel at the benefits. You must come to the reality that today's obstacles may be there tomorrow. Tomorrow may be a big day filled with stress and chaos. It does not matter. More than likely, you cannot change the events of tomorrow. But what you can change is how you approach them. And you will approach them as a Better New Person. You are establishing control. You are in Control!

RU NEW?

As you put your head on the pillow, put a smile on your face. Ask yourself the question, Am I New? Will I be New tomorrow? Get excited! Approach tomorrow as a glorious opportunity to grow into a New Person. *RU NEW?* Then shout it out, whether it be audibly or internally, I AM NEW!

It has been a glorious day. You are becoming a glorious person. You are New! Then close your eyes and you will sleep better today than you did yesterday. Good night

We have conquered the day-to-day, moment-to-moment, unavoidable struggles of normal daily life. Now, let's learn how to apply The New You to some specific aspects of life.

PART II

BEING NEW AND LIVING NEW

CHAPTER 3

THE CASH COW

CAREER

In your lifetime, you've encountered many people. During these encounters, people have asked questions to learn more about you. The questions are normally very generic. Questions like "where do you live?" "What is your name?" Depending on the activity, it may be a question such as "why are you here?" Or "where are you going?" But a very significant question usually arises. That question is, "what do you do?" For some, this question is a moment of joy and pride. You may be extremely happy about your career or your business. Or it may bring up negative thoughts and anxiety. Up to this point in your life, you probably have not really pondered your answer. Why is that? The answer is you respond based on yesterday and not today. Your response is dictated by the old you. But today, you are New. Your answer is based on today. You will answer with optimism and a path to success. You will not only be excited to answer the question, but you will also be ecstatic about where your career is going. You have a totally New Point of View. That view is not based on a moment ago or yesterday. It is now based on this moment and where you are going. You Are New!

The question asked, "What do you do?" is an opportunity for growth because you are practicing *The RU NEW Principles*. You may be just beginning your path in the work world. You may be starting a new job or going to school to train for a new career. You may be skilled labor or white-collar. Manual labor, a degreed professional, or any other opportunity that may have come your way doesn't matter. But, no matter what you have been doing for a career, you must realize that today is a New day. You are now applying The RU NEW Principles to enhance whatever you do to support yourself. So, when somebody asks you, "what do you do?" you will have a totally different attitude and response.

Why is that? Well, let's take a look at your career. You may have taken an opportunity that wasn't quite what you were planning on. You may not be happy with the choice that you were forced into. Like most people, you are probably dissatisfied. Therefore, yesterday you answered that question with regret, dissatisfaction, and a lack of optimism. You may be feeling that you are trapped in your present position. You cringe when somebody questions you about "what do you do for a living?"

But you now have triggers like sticky notes or reminders on your phone. You have utilized them for other aspects of your life. When your eyes open, you set your attitude for the day. You are perfecting the New You. You are New at home. You are New on your commute. But it's time to apply those principles to your career.

Before you leave home, you must ask the question *RU NEW?* Your answer must be, I AM NEW! No matter what yesterday brought into your life, today is a New day. Of course, that's easier said than done with some circumstances. Over time, you will know the level of effort needed to apply *The RU NEW Principles* to your work day. You have a New Weapon to combat yesterday's anxiety and displeasure. Today you're bringing in a totally New Attitude. Your outlook should be one of optimism and excitement because you have the opportunity to make changes in yourself and, ultimately, in your situation at work.

RU NEW?

The source of your discontent may be your supervisor. Or, it could be a coworker. It may be the task that you are required to do. You may feel that it is not fair. You may feel that you're not being treated fairly. Or, you may just hate what you are doing. But your destiny is in your hands. You must first change yourself. You must ask yourself as often as you need, *RU NEW?* That is the reset button. What angered you yesterday needs to be kept in mind. You must prepare for the same situation today. This is a New Day, and you are a New Person. How you handle the situation today will be far different and more beneficial than how it was handled yesterday.

Does this happen instantly? For some, it may. But for others, it takes work. This is not dependent on anyone but you. You are in control! You are a New You! Each day you will become a Better You. Each day you will handle stressful situations better than the day before. Each day you're getting to a Higher Level of New! You are a work in progress. But you must practice being New.

You must stop for just a second and take a deep breath when presented with a stressful situation. Whether it be audibly or internally, you must ask yourself, "RU NEW?" What does that mean? It means that you now have optimism and tolerance. You see the opportunity for growth. You begin to become excited when given stressful situations. You understand how much you are growing, and you begin to welcome the opportunity for growth. The stressful situations become your ally, not your enemy.

Your stress begins to decrease. You have less anxiety than yesterday. You are functioning at a higher level. Your eyes are beginning to open, and you're beginning to see opportunities you did not see yesterday. You may find the golden nugget in a pile of rocks. What you thought was a dead-end job now becomes an opportunity for advancement. It may be an opportunity to grow as a New Person. It may help you develop the skills necessary to make the changes in your life. It may transpire into a different career. Regardless if you continue your present career or decide to make a change, you'll be a far better person because You Are New. With that new attitude and outlook, you will begin to see opportunities for advancement. It may transpire into a raise. Or it may be that you become a happier person. But, if it turns out to be a change in career path, you are growing into a New Person that is more appealing to anyone or anything that is offering an opportunity.

When you walk in for your interview, your positive energy is evident. If you had walked in being the old you, your energies would be less prevalent and may be leaning towards the negative. Believe me, when interviewing an individual; you are able to pick up on both negative and positive energy. This may be the difference that distinguishes you from another candidate. Because You are New, the person interviewing you is less likely to have doubts. Less likely to question whether or not you are the person for the job. You will find that more doors will open, and there will be more opportunities in your path. Whether you are staying or going, you are becoming a wanted asset.

The RU NEW Principals will bring you happiness and reward. You will look forward to your workday. It may turn into more money in your pocket, resulting in a better lifestyle. Your coworkers will look forward to working with you. You will begin to be an influence on their attitudes. You may be instrumental in creating a New Person, which is extremely beneficial to you. In the perfect world, everyone would be on the same path. Is that possible? You will never know until you put forth the effort in being New and being an example for those around you.

You may ask what if it doesn't change the attitude of my coworkers or supervisor. Well, guess what? If they have not changed, you can now appreciate them for helping you become a New Person. They will be your springboard to a new career. Better yet, they are the reason for your Newfound Happiness. Or you can let them control you. You can let them dictate your attitude and allow them to be the reason for your anxiety. That is your choice. It has been said many times; You are in control. You Are New!

You have been pushing for a raise for a long time. Nothing that you have done up to this moment has resulted in your desired increase in pay. As the old saying states, "if you want changes in your life, you have to make changes in your life." You have been the old you up until today. Now you've made the changes. You are a New Person! They will feel the change, and they will see the benefits of the New You over time. They will become more receptive to you. They will be less likely to turn you down when you ask for that raise. There will be a stronger consideration for that promotion. This is all a result of Being New. What is it to be New? You will be less likely to react using negative emotions. You will be more tolerable of stressful situations. They will consider that the people you are dealing with are not New. You will be a person that everyone is looking forward to being around. You will become a superstar within the office. You will be accomplishing more than others. You will be advancing quicker. You may be the only individual in the office that's being considered for a promotion or rise. That is a product of your attitude, and that attitude is I

RU NEW?

Am New. You are conveying positive energy. You are being optimistic. You are not allowing the old you to surface. You are making changes in your life.

Tolerance is important as the New You comes to surface. As you begin believing that You Are New, you will begin to understand that not everyone is practicing The RU NEW Principles. You become tolerable. You have been where they are. You are no longer stagnant. You're moving forward. As you begin to master your craft, you will begin to tolerate the negative attitudes and laziness of those around you with less effort. The old you would allow them to anger you. The New You will be tolerable and thankful. Why are you thankful? You're thankful for the opportunity to grow. That individual who made your head explode in anger now becomes a valuable asset. They were controlling you. Now, you are controlling you! Because You Are New!

What if you are extremely happy with your present source of income? You may ask, "why do I need to change?" Understanding that a good thing can be better is the reason why you want to practice The RU NEW Principles. Your opportunities will be broader. Your monetary compensation could increase at a greater rate. You will build stronger relationships with people you may already have a good relationship with. Your supervisor will realize that you are indispensable. You will be a better person. You will be a New Person! The increasing positive energy will be extremely beneficial in the other aspects of your life.

There is absolutely no reason for you to stagnate. Becoming a better person, coworker or supervisor has a lasting positive effect on everyone in the workplace. You will bring home less stress and anxiety. We can always become better! Being the old you, reacting the old way, and being controlled by others, will result in the same outcome every time. So, ask yourself, "do I want a different outcome?" Of course, you do. Everyone does. It's time to make some changes. And that change is Being New.

But you are the supervisor. How you attained that position is irrelevant. Some may have worked hard for it. Others may have fallen into a good opportunity. You are held to higher expectations no matter how you attained that position. Results are expected. You must perform. You may be a new supervisor with very little skills in supervising. Or, you may be a veteran with plenty of skill. But, as a supervisor, you are under a microscope. Most are held to certain expectations. The bottom line performance is expected. *The RU NEW Principles* will definitely enhance your ability to perform. It will allow you to create results. This, possibly, will result in a higher position. It could result in bigger bonuses. You will have the ability to find quality people for your team. You will become the supervisor that everybody wants, the supervisor that everyone wants to work for.

More than likely, your performance is the reason for your present position. Do you have those moments where you feel stagnant? Do you ponder the reason why? Could it be economics? Or is it the level of talent within the hiring pool? Regardless of the reason for the stagnation, you are still in control. You are the captain of the ship. You steer its course. You can be the difference in a company's success or failure. Can you control economic conditions? For the most part, no, but you can be more successful in any economic condition. You have control of your team. You are the decision-maker. Being New is the most important decision you can make in a bad economic condition. A New Attitude filled with optimism. With a New Attitude, you will be able to retain and acquire better individuals for your team. You are creating a more productive and positive workplace. You are creating the desire for efficiency. Efficiency transpires into higher profit margins. Higher profit margins will make you an indispensable supervisor during poor economic conditions. But you must grow into a New Person. You must promote a New Attitude. The only way you can promote a New Attitude is to be New yourself.

Your task today is to find a new person for your team. You have a number of people coming in to interview. The old you would look only at skills and experience. I've known highly skilled people with years of experience, but they are the reason for discontent and anxiety within the team. Because You Are New, you will not only search for skill and experience, but you will be able to pinpoint and feel the positive energy within someone. On the other hand, if you are the old you, you may have an extremely skilled and experienced person with a positive attitude but decides to take another position. Why? Because the negative vibes you were projecting during the interview made them decide on a more positive opportunity. You must increase your value before you can increase the value of the workplace. You must become New!

What applies to a supervisor is tenfold for a business owner. As the owner of the business, everything rests on your shoulders. All the eyes are looking toward you. Their success or failure ultimately will fall upon you. That is not a fair fact. But it is true.

You are in constant decision mode. Your decisions have a direct impact on your business's success or failure. Your entire workforce will absorb a bad attitude and a lack of optimism and those you do business with. You can control both aspects. But first, you have to control you. You must be New every single day.

By using *The RU NEW Principles*, you will begin to transform the attitude of your business. Your business may already be very positive and optimistic. But it can always be better. You are the ultimate supervisor within your organization. You set the tone. You have a direct bearing on the attitudes of those individuals that are a contributing factor to both your successes and failures. The old you may be pretty darn good. There may be a positive work environment. Everyone may be optimistic. But everyone has those moments. And you will have those moments as well. There are old habits that will surface. It's not that they are bad or dangerous; it is that they can always be better. It can always be New!

RU NEW?

As you begin growing into a New Person, you will see the positive results in your personal life and your business. That will result in better relationships and a more successful business. You will see it in the profit and loss statement. You will see it in growth, both physically and monetarily. You will look at challenges from yesterday that brought anxiety and strife from a totally different viewpoint. Your New Attitude will cause you to welcome adversity. You will begin to look for new methods to handle old problems. You will look for new opportunities with an optimistic approach. In the past, you may have been too pessimistic about seeing the benefits of a new opportunity. Do not mistake pessimism for good business sense. Diving into a new opportunity blindly with optimism does not always transition into success. Your skills as a business owner and your business experience will always be invaluable. Your skills as a New

Person will only compound your business successes.

Those that you do business with will begin to see and feel the positive energy that you are gaining from *The RU NEW Principles*. Who you are doing business with and those that do business with you will have a stronger desire to continue the business relationship. You may have good business relationships already, but why would you not want to take them to a higher level? This will result in a more successful business. Success naturally will bring higher profit. Increased profit will benefit everyone working for you. It's a winning business approach. Do you want a more successful and profitable business? Of course, you do. Do you have a growing profitable business? Do you see increased profits? Do you object to faster growth and an increased profit percentage? Then I suggest that you begin asking yourself the question, *"RU NEW?"*

The RU NEW Principles are personal growth and increased self-image. They are tolerant, accepting, and optimistic, along with the expectation of a better day. It realizes that *everyone in your life is not using the RU NEW Principles.* But they should. They could. They will! It is a different outlook for the growth and success of your business. They are better personal relationships. Your life is getting less stressful. Moments of anxiety become less stifling. You are finding inner peace, and everyone benefits from that. You begin every day asking yourself, *"RU NEW?"* And you are shouting it from the mountain tops, "I AM NEW!" You will begin to see the results, but why stop there?

Your successes are becoming more numerous. You are becoming more profitable. But why on earth would you hide this from your team? Why would you limit your success? Do you object to exponential success and profits? Of course, you don't. The RU NEW Principles have resulted in a better you and a more successful business. Now let's compound those successes.

Why would you promote *The RU NEW Principles* to your team? Plainly said, they will be excited about their future within your company. Once they begin practicing *The RU NEW Principles*, their personal and work lives will be enhanced. You make constant investments into your company. So why not make the *RU NEW* Investment in your team? It will benefit not only you but everybody associated with you. By encouraging your team to practice *The RU NEW Principles*, you will be investing in your business's success and their lives. It will create a happier workplace. It will promote optimism. It will encourage active participation. They will be far more excited to be a part of this team. Their demeanor will change. There will be fewer anxiety-related problems. You will see decreased sick days. You will see more productivity and your profits will increase. Increased profits will give you another tool to retain your valuable team members. Your business is now growing in leaps and bounds.

How do you promote *The RU NEW Principles* within your business workplace? It first begins with You. You must be the cornerstone. You have to be the example. By them seeing a New You, they will definitely be curious. Their curiosity will be an open door. Promote it with action and satisfy their curiosity verbally. First, promote *The RU NEW Principles* for their personal life. Share with them how *The RU NEW Principles* have benefited your life. Once they see the benefits in their personal life, they will be able to apply them to their work life.

RU NEW?

You will be amazed at the difference it will make in your business.

The most beneficial factor in every work or business environment known to man is attitude. *The RU NEW Principles* will build your business, your lifestyle, and your attitude about life.

So I asked the question once again, "RU NEW? Are They New? Is your Business New?"

If you can answer these questions with a BIG YES, you will begin to see an amazing change in every aspect of your life! Including your career or business!

So shout it as loud as you can

"I AM NEW!"

CHAPTER 4

PLAY NICE WITH OTHERS

RELATIONSHIPS

Everyone has different priorities in life. One of the keys to having a healthy relationship is to understand not only your priorities but the priorities of those individuals in your life. You must make allowances for the differences. In order to accomplish this, you must have a New Attitude. Ask yourself, "RU NEW?" By being New, you will begin to have tolerance. With a New Attitude, you will understand their priorities' magnitude. The old you normally would focus only on your own priorities. By being New, you will begin to understand that compromise is very important for a healthy relationship. You may be that individual that already has the right mindset. As it is true for any aspect of your life, there is room for improvement. You may be that individual that is set in your ways. You may refuse to realize that your priorities are not always everyone else's priorities. By becoming New, you will begin to see a difference in your relationships. This is due to your New found tolerance. There are many moments in life that will attempt to make you revert back to the old you. By practicing *The RU NEW Principles*, you will become less likely to give into that old frame of mind.

There are those moments that will make you lock your heels in. Then, of course, you will allow the old you to dictate your actions. But you must ask yourself at that moment, "Do I want to be New? Am I willing to have a New Attitude.? Do I want the same strained relationship? Or do I want a New and Exciting Relationship?

Do you have the tools to make this happen? Yes, you do! You have *The RU NEW Principles*. They will allow you to have more fulfilling relationships. But you must practice your craft. You have to work on yourself first. Then you can concentrate on those around you. Without being *NEW*, you will more than likely revert back to the old you. Back to having the same relationship issues of the past. You so badly want that relationship to change today and forever. Then you must be *NEW*!

Are you in that precarious moment that causes you anger, anxiety, and turmoil? You must control yourself and ask the question, "*RU NEW?*". Take a deep breath and focus on the New You. Understand that you are a work in progress, and this will take effort. You may be angered. You may be overwhelmed with anxiety. No matter your state of mind, you must allow yourself to be NEW. Your viewpoint must change. You must realize that the change is for the better. You don't always have to get your way. Sometimes the change will ultimately transform into a new viewpoint that is now very acceptable.

As you become the New Better You, you will begin to see a decrease in your anxiety and discontent. Remember, you are in control. Do not allow the moment or the person to dictate your Newness. Do not allow them to force you into the habits of the old you. Know that you are controlling the situation. You are controlling yourself. Once you have both in control, you will begin to believe that you are a New Person. YOU ARE NEW!

Your friends are coming over today. But your significant other has different priorities today. Is either priority right or wrong? In your mind, you may find fault in their priority and vice versa. Neither is wrong. You may lock your heels in and say that you are going to see your friends today no matter what. The other individual involved may do the same. That may work out, but under normal circumstances, this does create some animosity. You may have given very little thought to the significance of your decision. You may have focused solely on your priorities. But now that You Are New, you will begin to understand that a healthy relationship requires constant transformation. In the beginning, you will resist. That is the old you fighting to retain control. You must be persistent in the transformation into the New You. You must stop, take a breath and ask yourself the question, "RU NEW? Do I believe I can be New? How will my life and relationships improve by practicing The RU NEW Principles?"

If you want relationship growth, you must ask yourself these questions in every situation. What are we trying to accomplish here? Well, that answer can be very simple and complicated at the same time. We're trying to change our viewpoint. We're trying to change our attitude. The attitude we use in a relationship's tense moments can be very detrimental or rewarding. So, you have to decide if the change is worthwhile. Do you want a better relationship? It is hard for me to be convinced by anyone that they have no interest in better relationships. Therefore, unless you have some strange desire to have horrible relationships, you must make the changes necessary to become The New You. Over time, you will find that the energy you are conveying to the individual in this relationship will begin to transform them into a New Person as well. They will become more tolerating of your priorities. Unknowingly, they will begin to be New. You will find that tolerance and compromise will become a two-way street. You will begin to see a change in your methods for handling almost every situation. You will no longer revert back to chaos and strife. You will find contentment. This contentment will give you a softer approach toward other people's priorities. You will begin to feel less anxious. There will be a newfound joy in your life. And your relationships will definitely improve!

Understand that most people's nature will lean towards the selfish side. That does include you. That is human nature. But a selfish nature is deeply rooted in the past. As a New You, you do not rely on the past to dictate today or tomorrow. Instead, you allow your New Attitude and *The RU NEW Principles* to transform you into a less selfish individual. Over time you'll find that a selfish reaction that you may revert to will give you anxiety. When that moment happens, you must shout with joy that you are excited about the transformation into the New You. It is a test of your progress. If you are no longer comfortable with a selfish approach, you will realize that the transformation has begun.

In the days of the old you, there were individuals in your life that you dreaded encountering. Some of these individuals you could avoid. That would have been a highly recommended practice when you were the old you. But now that You Are New, you have an opportunity for growth! You have an opportunity to practice being The New You. Understand that all of the encounters, the words said, or the actions of yesterday do not guarantee the outcome of today. Don't get me wrong; there are individuals that will be miserable no matter what. For some unknown reason, they have decided to be miserable. Miserable people want to be with other miserable people. Because You Are New, there is no reason to avoid these individuals. There is no reason to feel anxiety about an encounter. You should be excited about the opportunity to grow as The New You. You should be extremely excited about the lessons you will learn from this miserable person. Another positive aspect of being New is that you may actually transform that miserable person into a curious individual. Their curiosity is being drawn out due to the positive energy of you being New. You may be instrumental in their change. You may help them to be less miserable. They will find less joy in trying to make your life miserable. Over time, they will begin to understand that they no longer have power over your attitude. They will understand that they are wasting energy towards an unattainable goal. They will begin to focus on the New You. Deep down in their soul, they will begin to be curious. They will enjoy absorbing your New Positive Energy. They will begin to seek a better relationship with you. So, there it is. You have control of the situation. You have control of yourself. And you are beginning to have control of the attitudes of those individuals around you. You no longer need to be anxious about those encounters. You begin to realize that you can transform the encounters. Your relationships become better. As you get to a Higher Level of New, you begin to control those encounters immediately.

Absolutely no one in your life should be in control of your attitude. No one should be able to decide whether or not You Are New!

Social interactions are unlimited and unavoidable. You cannot avoid social interactions unless you live alone on a deserted island. All social interactions are relationship based. The ability to control your attitude during these encounters is a very beneficial skill. You now have a very effective tool called *The RU NEW Principals*. With this invaluable tool in your belt, you are better prepared to handle any relationship-based interaction. Learn how to use it. Become a master of your craft. But any master continuously hones their skills. If you have social anxiety and are using *The RU NEW Principles*, you should be excited about venturing into the world. That world could be your home life. It is definitely your interaction in your career or business. It is your interaction with your significant other and possibly children. Your family, your friends, we could go on and on and on. Therefore, every interaction is a relationship.

You will be better at building relationships, or should I say positive relationships, when you apply *The RU NEW Principles*. Up to this point, you have utilized your experiences of the past, whether they were positive or negative, to determine how a relationship will be. Now that You Are New, you can approach every encounter as a new relationship regardless of how long you have known that person. Don't get me wrong, your interactions in the past with individuals should be kept in mind. But the judgment should be far less. Remember the principle that good people are capable of bad things and bad people are capable of good things. A bad relationship can be better, but a good relationship can be great.

When you wake in the morning, you put your *RU NEW Armer* on—knowing that when you walk through that threshold, you will be given the opportunity to build positive, rewarding relationships. You should be excited. In the beginning, you may be apprehensive. Rightfully so, you are building the New You. You will become more optimistic as each day passes. Your skills will be fine-tuned. You will look forward to every social interaction. Every day you are at a Higher Level of New!

Let's talk about one of the most important relationships in your life. Your relationship with your significant other. For some, this relationship takes the least amount of work. That is absolutely wonderful. But remember what was said, a good thing can be better. For some, the relationship with their significant other can have trials. To get through these trials, you have relied on the old you. This may be the cause of the repeat moments of trials and tribulations. Some relationships are in constant turmoil. Others are in periodic turmoil. Regardless of what applies to you, it can get better. In the past, you have relied on advice from other people. You may have relied on counseling. You may have read a few books on relationships. But, nowhere have you been given *The RU NEW Principles.* Usually, the advice given by individuals that we trust is given with good intentions. It may be great advice. But on occasion, the advice can actually cause more harm to the relationship than you want.

Remember, you are in control. You have the ability to control yourself, and you can be influential in the attitude of the individuals in your life. That said, relying solely on advice from people that mean well could be helpful or harmful. I'm not saying to disregard advice from those people who care about you. What I am saying is that you must get yourself in control first. You have to create a New You. Once you have created the New You, you will be able to distinguish between good advice and bad. If you are questioning yourself, why on earth would you rely on someone else who does not know the inner turmoil that you are going through. One of the most beneficial attributes that you can have is self-control. You must have yourself under control before you can control the relationship.

Think back to the day's past. Remember how you reacted to stressful moments within a relationship. It may have been with anger or sadness. It may have been a moment of extreme anxiety. These are all emotions that come from a lack of self-control. Emotion is one of the strongest influencers in deciding as it pertains to relationships. Sometimes, we just need to cry. I understand that completely. Sometimes anger is unavoidable. The moment may dictate a bundle of emotions. We are emotional creatures. That is human nature. But we have to exercise a certain amount of control of our emotions. Our emotions can overwhelm us, causing us to make bad decisions as far as it pertains to relationships. Just because something comes to mind in an emotional moment doesn't mean that it has to be spoken. Sometimes we need to install a filter. Up to this point, that filter has been restrained. Under many circumstances, restraint is difficult. But today, you have a new filter, and that filter is "I Am New!"

RU NEW?

You may be saying that this principle is merely looking at the brighter side. Well, there is some accuracy in your judgment. That could be very helpful in most situations. But just looking at the brighter side may be very difficult. Some situations may be difficult to find that brighter side. Today that has changed. In those moments where there is difficulty in finding a brighter side, you will now find the brighter side within you. Why? Because You Are New! You have a greater ability to handle all situations because you're not relying on the old you. What is meant by relying on the old you is that you more than likely have relied strictly on emotion and the advice of others; without making strides in your personal growth, or should I say you're Newness, the old you will make decisions that will bring about the same results. The old you was yesterday. Today You Are New. You will handle relationship problems with a different outlook. You will be better at building relationships!

Your relationship is having a moment. You may be arguing over finances. It may be the kids. It may be immediate family or career choices. It may be something of extreme significance or as insignificant as someone didn't throw the trash. No matter the subject matter of the disagreement, you must pause for a moment and reflect. There are two reflections that you must ponder. One is the decisions of yesterday. Those decisions were made by the old you. Some may be positive; others may be negative. But that was the old you. You must become New. You must ask yourself, *"RU NEW?"* How much have you grown? Have you used the positive outcomes of the past as a learning moment? You must ponder the negative outcomes as well. The old you have a tendency to make the same decisions that will cause continued difficulties.

RU NEW?

Relying on the old you will cause you to react the same as you did in the past. Remember that saying, "if you are reacting the same way, how can you expect a different outcome?" The New You will bring about a positive outcome. You are learning tolerance and acceptance. You have more understanding and compassion. You have control of yourself and newfound confidence. You are now looking at this moment from a totally different perspective.

Unless the issue is extreme and would be a dealbreaker, you must use *The RU NEW Principles* as the solution. You must have a New Outlook. You must find new ways to resolve situations. But first, you have to rectify situations within you. That means getting rid of the old you and becoming New. Now you will approach a relationship problem with a far better attitude.

RU NEW?

For most couples, the beginning of a relationship is one that is, of course, brand new. It's full of excitement and optimism. You must remember what that felt like. You were excited about sharing your life with your significant other. You were concentrating more on the positive attributes instead of picking them apart. You were not focused on the negative. Your relationship was New! Can you see how being New can rejuvenate your relationship? You must use *The RU NEW Principles* every opportunity you can find. You must rejuvenate that relationship. With one of you being New, then one of you is bringing excitement and optimism into the relationship once again. Are You New? You are now allowing your relationship to be New again. What you will find in most cases is that they will draw from your positive energy. That will begin to open their eyes. The change will be miraculous as they begin to fill with positive energy. You have grown, and they are growing. Who knows, you may be the cause of them becoming New. Then there is a 100% chance for a positive outcome.

Are you beginning to understand how *The RU NEW Principles* work? As you get better at being New, the New You will begin to influence others. I am not saying that these principles are an absolute resolution to every issue in your relationship. What I am saying is by applying *The RU NEW Principles* to your relationship, you will give it a far greater chance to succeed. Once you understand the foundation and begin your journey of Being New, you will not only see a difference in your relationships at home but in every relationship in your life.

So why would you revert back to the old you knowing that the New and Improved You will reap many positive results? Well, human nature and society will do their best to make you fall back into a path that will bring the same old result. It is up to you to make the change. Nobody can make the change for you. You have a decision to make. That decision is based on the simple question, "do I want a better relationship?" Well, do you?

Do you want your relationship to be better? Do you want an exciting, rejuvenated relationship? Do you want it to Be New? Are You NEW? Then, what are you waiting for? Pick up *The RU NEW Principles* and run with it! You owe it to yourself and your significant other! *RU NEW?* Is your relationship New?

Hold Hands and Say,

WE ARE NEW!!!!

CHAPTER 5

MAN, I FEEL GOOD

HEALTH

So far, we have concentrated on You Being New as it pertains to your external world. Now it's time to talk about the internal. We have seen the huge impact of being New on your social interactions, relationships, and your source of income. But being New has an enormously positive effect on your physical and mental health.

Chances are, you are beginning your journey of Being New. That assumption is due to the fact that you are reading this book. On the other hand, you may already be part of *The New Nation* and practicing the principles. Regardless of what level of New you are, *The RU NEW Principles* will positively impact your health.

RU NEW?

As you begin to grow into a Brand New You, your stress levels will begin to decrease. It is a proven fact that stress has an enormous impact on your health, both mental and physical. You no longer wake up and step into the mindset of the old you. If you are using your triggers and reminders to focus on a positive mindset, your attitude is conducive to reducing stress and anxiety. In addition, you will find that you are sleeping better. Good sound sleep is vital for a Healthy New You. Waking rested and putting on the Armor of Being New will start your day on a positive track to Better Health.

Last night, you put your head on your pillow, not feeling your best physically. Before you drifted into sleep, you should have practiced *The RU NEW Principles*. By going to bed New, you will sleep more soundly, and your sleep will be deeper. The body has to rejuvenate. The quality of sleep determines the level of rejuvenation.

RU NEW?

Your thoughts will determine your quality of sleep prior to falling asleep. By getting a sound night of sleep combined with the Practice of Being New, you'll find that your health will improve. It doesn't take a Ph.D. to understand this. There are countless studies in the medical field that proves quality sleep is conducive to good health. That is the first step to becoming the New Healthy You.

Every person that you encounter can expose you to the potential of sickness. Our body is meant to be exposed to bacteria, viruses, and germs. We are taught that this is our natural method of building our immune system. But if our immune system is not strong enough, we will have to deal with the illness. This is where a strong body and mind become a huge factor in dealing with the illness. And *The RU NEW Principles* will be beneficial. Why? Have you ever heard the term "you will worry yourself sick"? We have all had a moment during sickness when all we could focus on was how bad we felt. We are all guilty. But this does nothing to speed your recovery. Sometimes we are forced to seek medical help. We're given medication that is very beneficial to our recovery. On the other hand, there are times that we are just so hardheaded that we refuse to see a medical professional. We feel that our body will heal itself. We have proven that to ourselves on an occasion or two. There are two key factors at work here, Physical and mental condition.

If your focus is merely on the sickness, that is negative energy. Negative energy is a product of stress. Stress has a negative impact on both our minds and body. Today You Are New. Yes, you are sick. There is a struggle going on inside of you. It's not just the physical attributes of the sickness; it is the attitude you have towards your recovery. You must practice *The RU NEW Principles!*

RU NEW?

It is time to ask yourself, "*RU NEW?*" It is also time to ask yourself if you have control of your mental state. Do you have the attitude that is beneficial to kicking the sickness? By being The New You, yes, you do! Having a New Attitude will produce positive energy. Positive energy will make your mental state more receptive towards your recovery. Having a negative attitude will increase your stress levels. Increasing your stress levels will make you feel worse. Your body is an amazing machine. Yes, you can worry yourself sick. When you are sick, you can increase the time of recovery. That is the old you. You need to stop focusing on the sickness. You must concentrate on the recovery. That is being the New You!

You cough, or maybe you sneeze. You have a scratchy throat or maybe the sniffles. The old you would immediately begin down the negative path. You would assume that this was the onset of sickness. That is the negative approach toward your body's ability to fight off illness. You inventory your symptoms and assume the worse. Before you're actually sick, you're beginning to feel sick. This is the attitude of the old negative you. Your mind may begin to wander. A wandering mind focused on negativity will create stress. A stressful body is more susceptible to illness.

But now You Are New! You will stop assuming that you are becoming sick. You will stop worrying yourself being sick. Yes, you need to monitor your symptoms. Some symptoms are more severe than others. If your symptoms linger for an extended period of time, it's time to use common sense. Consult your physician. What needs to be kept in mind is you are pushing positive energy toward a potential ailment by using *The RU NEW Principles*. If the ailment is unavoidable, at least you will have a positive attitude. That will be instrumental in a speedier recovery.

Remember, You Are New! You are programming your mental state. Your attitude will change towards your physical and mental health. When You Are New, your body will respond differently. Remember, positive energy brings about positive results. Do not assume anything. The old you would assume the worst. You were generating negative energy. What does negative energy create? Of course, Negative results, Your mental health will be improved during the course of this ailment. You will find fewer unneeded trips to the physician. You will find recovery times shortened. And you will find your mental health improving.

For the less fortunate that suffer from chronic pain, *The RU NEW Principles* will be extremely beneficial. Chronic pain is a test of one's mind, body, and soul. Every day is a test of one's willpower. Every day you struggle with your attitude. And that is to be expected. The struggle takes a toll on your body and soul. Every day seems to be a continuation of the previous days. The only thing that changes is your increasing negativity.

So now it's time to shed the old you. It's time to make some changes. Changes to your mental approach to dealing with your condition. This condition may be temporary, long-lasting, or permanent. Regardless of which applies, it is time to change your attitude. Easier said than done, right? Yes, exactly. But if you want things to change, you must begin changing your attitude. Your attitude may be instrumental in your recovery. But even if your condition is permanent, you can change your attitude. And that will give you a Higher Quality of Life! You must look at every moment as an opportunity to create a positive mental attitude. You must ask yourself if you want to be New. You must ask yourself if you want to improve your quality of life. You must ask yourself, *"RU NEW?"*

As you become New, your energy will become increasingly more positive. As your energies become more positive, your ability to handle the pain will increase. As your abilities grow, so will you. You are becoming New! You will be able to handle your situation better. As your confidence in your New ability increases, so will your tolerance for the pain. And with tolerance, your quality of life will improve.

No one is saying that this will be easy. But what choices do you have? Well, there are two choices. One, you can remain the old you and have a negative outlook on your condition. Or, you can become a New You and generate positive energy. The old you will not help you at all. The New You will take every step necessary to improve your quality of life. If this condition is temporary, your positive energy may be instrumental in creating a quicker recovery time. If your condition is permanent, then your goal has to be to improve your quality of life. Not just in body but also in mind and soul. Your task is to become an improved you. You are creating a New Attitude. This will divert your focus from doom and despair to hope and optimism. You will be increasing your positive energy and replacing the negative. Thus, creating an improved quality of life. You can do this! You are in control! You can make the necessary changes. Ask yourself every opportunity that you have "RU NEW?". Believe it deep in your soul. Every moment of every day will be an opportunity to be the New You. Each moment will be an opportunity to be New at a Higher Level. You are now building your ability to handle your situation. You are capable! It's up to you. Believe in yourself, and you will definitely be *NEW!*

Now that You Are New, your quality of life has changed. Who knows, maybe the impossible and permanent will miraculously become possible and temporary. The majority of our abilities are unknown. The mind is a powerful thing. By becoming New, you may uncover that one avenue that changes permanent into temporary. You now have hope! Your mind is generating positive energy! With this New Positive Energy, you may unlock an ability that you and no one else realized was capable of. You must remain positive. You must remain *NEW!*

Have you heard it said that stress would take years off your life? We all have. We have heard this from experts in the medical field. Then why wouldn't you believe them? Stress is a product of your environment compounded by your methods of handling it. The old you are more stressed and anxious. That was yesterday. Today, You Are New! You are in control of reducing your stress. You are practicing *The RU NEW Principles!* You will not allow anyone or anything to control your attitude. You are in Control!

So, you have recovered. Now, it's time to head out into the world feeling 10 times better, both physically and mentally. You will be exposed to people who will tell you all about their ailments. They will tell you about every ache and pain that they have. The old you would absorb this energy and usually discard it shortly thereafter. But on occasion, you would allow it to transform your mental attitude towards ailments and attitude. As the old saying proclaims, "we become the people we associate with."

So, you're listening to your coworker. They tell you a story. A story about someone they know who had a dull pain in the center of their chest. They ignored the symptom. Then the story ends with the individual having a heart attack and passing away. Your mind is absorbing the facts of the story. Yes, you should listen to your body. But do not be completely consumed with every small tinge of pain. You know your body. You know when something is wrong. And when you do, I highly suggest you see your physician.

I will share a personal story. For a period of time, I had a dull ache in the center of my chest. Because I was hardheaded, I decided to put off going to see my physician. Well, late one night, the pain became strong. I was the old me. I began to think I had a heart attack. I started feeling extremely anxious. My heart rate began to increase, and my blood pressure was rising. I asked my wife to call 911. By the time the medical professionals reached me, my blood pressure was 220/120 and climbing. I was given an injection to relax me. They put me in the ambulance and drove down my long driveway. I remember seeing my home and a street light as we turned onto the highway. Then, I honestly believed that this was going to be the last time I would see my home and my family.

I woke up in the hospital with a doctor at my side. The doctor explained to me that I was not having a heart attack or a stroke. As a matter of fact, he said that he really did not know what was wrong with me. He said that the increase in blood pressure was likely due to stress and anxiety. Boy, was that an eye-opener. Yes, eventually, it was found that I had a bacteria in my stomach that was causing the pain. But I learned a very valuable lesson. Your mind can make you sick. Your lack of mental control could possibly kill you. Yes, it was an eye-opener. I began transforming myself. I had a totally different outlook about life. and I Began becoming the New Me!

RU NEW?

I wake up every morning and look in the mirror. I ask myself every day, "*RU NEW?*" Before I drift to sleep every evening, I remind myself that I Am New by asking the question and shouting internally *I AM NEW!* My health has been far better. I attribute that to taking care of my body, of course. But I now take care of my mind. I have transformed myself into The New Me.

On occasion, I have had the same dull pain in my stomach area. And yes, it did try to revert me back to the old me. But I refused! I knew that it was from the damage of the bacteria from the past. If I let my mind take over, I may have wound up right back in the hospital again. When I feel the pain, I remind myself I Am New! Don't get me wrong; if the pain had not subsided, I would have gone to see my physician. Amazingly I drank a little water and had something to eat, and the pain went away. That's right; I was hungry. I was not having a heart attack. I refused to let my mind take over and put me back into that same terrible situation I was in years back. This is the power of *The RU NEW Principles!* I am living proof that these Principles work! No, I am not a medical professional. But I am a man that has overcome obstacles by utilizing *The RU NEW Principles.* And I am compelled to share that with you.

So I ask you....

"RU NEW?"

CHAPTER 6

I'M A NERVOUS WRECK

ANXIETY

Anxiety. This is a life changer. Anxiety affects your life and everyone else in your life. In some cases, it may be the controlling factor of someone's entire life. Anxiety is merely a byproduct of stress. Anxiety shows up in many forms and varies in magnitude.

Remember that individual or situation at work discussed in previous chapters? It may be the first thought on your mind when you wake. It may begin when you show up at work. It is definitely there during your work day. It may be interaction with family. Practically every situation in our life will spawn a certain level of anxiety. The fear of the unknown or the fear of failure. It may be a feeling of inadequacy or a feeling of being overbearing. As said, practically everything in our lives brings about a certain level of anxiety.

You may be that individual that says you have no anxiety in your life. I challenge you. You say there is no anxiety, and I can appreciate your optimism. The fact is, we are exposed to the uncomfortable situation every single day of our lives. Our ability to control our actions and reactions is dependent on coping mechanisms. You may be that individual that can handle pretty much any situation. But, can you honestly say that you feel no different when confronted with an uncomfortable situation? Is there a mild exhilaration? Is there a heightened sense of awareness? Do you breathe a little faster? Is your heart rate somewhat elevated? These are your internal coping mechanisms.

The fortunate individual has strong enough internal coping abilities to overcome practically any situation that may cause high levels of anxiety for others. However, there are those moments, even for the strongest, that may cause a reaction that may not produce the most desired results. Those undesirable results will cause a level of anxiety. Therefore, we all suffer from some level of anxiety.

There are various levels of social anxiety. All of us suffer from social anxiety. It may be a party that you are invited to, and you only know the host. For some, they are considered social butterflies. The opposite personality is sometimes referred to as antisocial. No matter where you fall between the two, there is a level of social anxiety. It may come from the need for acceptance, or it may come strictly from the fear of rejection. The social butterfly is searching for acceptance; so is the other end of the spectrum. Rejection is brutal. For those that handle rejection well, there is still a level of anxiety involved. Although the discomfort of rejection may be momentary, it is still there. It can be brutal for those with a lack of coping skills in the social environment.

Your anxiety may be health-related. Your anxiety may be the cause of your health situation. Health and longevity have a high priority for everyone on this earth. When we are sick, we experience many forms of anxiety; the anxiety of losing money, the anxiety of your coworkers having to cover for you. Not knowing the cause of your illness can create anxious moments. Those with life-changing medical conditions deal with extreme levels of anxiety. Change in lifestyle, having to depend on another. Not knowing how long this condition will persist. High levels of anxiety can come from not knowing if you will survive this condition.

Your relationship, your marriage, or your next-door neighbor. Your career or your business. Your physical and mental health. Your finances or the lack of. Your children and your family. We can make a list a mile long! Practically every event and aspect of our life will create some form of anxiety.

For some people with extreme anxiety, their life will be completely focused on the anxiety. This can be crippling. Extremely anxious moments can create panic attacks. Panic attacks can affect your health. It can affect every aspect of your life. Personally, as mentioned in the previous chapter, it can drive you to the brink of death. And that's extremely scary! However, anxiety is nothing to discount. Anxiety takes years off of your life. It can destroy a relationship. For those with high levels of anxiety, your daily life is dictated by the intensity of every anxious situation. For those with lower levels of anxiety, it still has an effect on you and those around you.

So, I challenge you. Think back to a moment in your life that was uncomfortable. Think about how you were feeling up until that moment. Then realize that your demeanor had changed. Your attitude had changed. It may have been momentary, or it may have been long-lasting. Regardless, your mindset has changed. We all experience anxiety. This is without argument. It is there, and we usually cannot change that. We all experience stressful and uncomfortable situations. But what is important is how we deal with those situations.

Whether you deal with extreme or mild anxiety, there is a tool that will help you deal with anxiety far better than anything you have ever tried. That tool is The RU NEW Principles! There is the old you and soon-to-be New You! Whether you have been practicing these principles for a time or this is the first that you have heard of these principles, you will be able to handle your anxiety far better than you ever have. How you coped with those situations in the past is the old you. Now, You Are New!

You are anxious due to your experience. Your experience of life so far. The intensity is determined by the level of discomfort during previous episodes. Each occurrence of anxiety is usually stronger than the last if not addressed. You may have tried various methods to rectify your condition; mental exercise, physical exercise, alcohol, medication (Legal or otherwise), or you may have given up and decided to become numb to the condition by ignoring your condition.

All of the attempts to rectify have been based on the experiences of yesterday. That was the old you. Today You Are New! You will venture out into the world, the anxiety-causing world, with a new outlook and hope. You are now strapping on the armor based on The RU NEW Principles! You have a newfound direction! There is hope! So now, let's learn how to battle this demon called anxiety!

You know that feeling—that moment when you're placed into an uncomfortable situation. You can feel it beginning to well up inside of you. In the past, you may have had difficulty identifying the onset of an anxiety attack. The moment may be mild, or it could be severe. Regardless, you have to identify the onset of anxiety by calling it what it is. It is a trigger.

It begins with that warm sensation. Some are mild, and others will cause you to sweat. You may start out a little lite headed or just plain disoriented. Your stomach may be queasy, or you may be just plain sick to your stomach. Everyone is different. It does not matter what your symptoms are. This is the onset of anxiety.

What matters is being able to identify it when it raises its ugly head. You've been triggered.

Yesterday, you either overcame it relatively easily, or it completely overwhelmed you. If you were fortunate, it passed quickly. But you did nothing to address the trigger. Only to have it return again. If you were not so fortunate, the anxiety probably overcame you and ruined your entire day. Regardless, if it was a minor or a major event, you more than likely did not identify the trigger.

What is "the trigger"? It is a situation. It is a person or memory. It may be a passing thought. But, it is a significant moment that triggers your anxiety. This is the front line of the battleground! You have to get good at anticipating a trigger. If you can see it coming, you will have more control. This is where you stand your ground!

RU NEW?

Remember why you are doing this. Not only will it make your life better, but it will also have less of an effect on those around you. You are conscientious about how your anxiety affects your loved ones and friends. But, by identifying the onset of an anxiety attack, you will be able to enlighten your people. They will begin to understand the triggers and will be able to help you better. Your friends and family care about you and would like nothing more than to see you overcome the issues of anxiety.

Now, you have become proficient at identifying the triggers. Your friends and family have become more proficient at identifying them as well. Now, let's get ready to rumble! Let's take control! Let's make your life better! How? Why? Because You Are New!

The triggers of your anxiety are out of your control. They are someone or something that sets you off. You may be able to control your interactions with some people or have limited control of your surroundings. But why live your life in seclusion? Why have you avoided people and situations? The answer is that you feel like you are not in control. That is the old you. But now You Are New!

Remember the discussion at the beginning of the book where you created triggers? A sticky note or an object. They are designed for you to take a right first step when your eyes open in the morning. And we discussed the same for practically every activity during your day. This new trigger will also help you beat back those anxious situations.

There was a gentleman that I was fortunate to meet. We exchanged small talk. He began talking about his family. He explained to me that his 13-year-old daughter suffered from serious moments of anxiety. Her anxiety was affecting the family. He stated that they tried practically everything they could think of to no avail. I saw the need to share The RU NEW Principles with him. I explain to him that these principles are unlike anything he has tried. It focuses on transforming the old person that she is into a New Person. We discussed triggers, and he explained to me that she had many. He said that her anxiety attacks have, on occasion, turned into panic attacks. It has been going on long enough that they are able to see the onset of anxiety. I explained that The RU NEW Principles are not only psychological, but they are also physical. By utilizing the RU NEW Triggers, she will be using a physical object to help her psychologically. I encouraged him to buy a locket or a medallion. In the locket or on the medallion to inscribe "RU NEW?" That was the first step.

The physical object alone will do nothing but make her happy about receiving a gift. But understanding what the object symbolizes and how to use it would be very beneficial in helping overcome her anxiety issues. She must understand that the anxiety that she had yesterday cannot be changed. What can be changed is how she overcomes this condition today. She must remember that the methods used yesterday did not accomplish the ultimate goal. That is the past, and that is the old her.

She needs to understand that she can control this. That we have control at a level that most do not understand. What is causing the anxiety comes from within her. She needs to understand that she has ultimate control. She needs to build confidence. She needs to believe in herself. She needs to believe that She is New!

Today is a new day. Today you are in control. You are beginning to identify the triggers. And now you have your own personal RU NEW Trigger to fight back!

RU NEW?

The conversation continued. We discussed how to utilize his daughter's New Trigger. A medallion or a locket. I shared my contact information with him. A few days later, he sent me a text message that he shared what we discussed with his wife and daughter. They were extremely excited. He stated that his daughter had a Newfound optimism and belief that she could manage her anxiety.

The RU NEW Principles give anyone the optimism to handle whatever situation that is in front of them. It is a new frame of mind. It's a new consciousness. It is the New You! Being New gives one a whole New Outlook on Life. You now have your own powerful personal reset button! The RU NEW Principles will give you a New Lease on Life!

Now let's talk about how to use the RU NEW Triggers. It is something that needs to be practiced. It has to be used. You have to understand that these principles work. Up to this point, you have used whatever it is to cope with your anxiety. It may be working. But the addition of The RU NEW Principles will make it even better. If what you have been doing has not been working for you, then it's time to make a change. And that change is to Become New!

There you are. You just woke up to the chaos of home life. You're driving in the concrete jungle. You are wallowing in the stress of gainful employment. You are enthralled in a disagreement with your significant other or your family. You are struggling with fatigue and sickness. This book is not long enough to go through every scenario you may face. They all trigger anxiety. Plainly said, every person and event in your life can create anxiety for you.

No matter the situation, you must identify the potential for anxiety. Then, once it begins to well up in you, you need to secure your trigger.

What is used as a trigger is up to you. Personally, I use reminders on my phone. I put sticky notes in strategic places. But, the most important trigger is the one I carry with me every day, all day. It is a small cloth bag that has a couple of small items personally important to me. One of those items is a medallion that has "I Am New!" inscribed on it.

Whether you are new to The RU NEW Principles or have been practicing the principles for quite some time, you must never quit utilizing your Triggers. Stress and anxiety will always try to abuse you. If you have been using The RU NEW Principles for a period of time, you are definitely seeing the positive results. If not, it's time to begin creating the habits of utilizing your Triggers. Regardless of your level, you will continue seeing positive results. If you are like me, you are definitely interested in having a better day today and every day after.

RU NEW?

Are you interested in less anxiety? Do you want to increase your quality of life? Then utilizing The RU NEW Principles will continuously produce better results.

So, there it is. You feel it coming. You ask yourself, Are You New? You answer, Yes, I Am NEW! Now, if you are worried about people thinking that you are crazy, you may want to do this internally instead of audibly. But, realistically, I could care less. So, you reach into your pocket or your purse. You grab your necklace that says, "I Am New!" You repeat to yourself; I Am New! as many times as you need to. As you grow in The RU NEW Principles, it will eventually decrease to one question and answer.

Repeat as needed:

"RU NEW? Yes, I Am New! RU NEW? I Am New! I Am in Control because I Am New!

RU NEW?

What controlled me yesterday has no control today! Yesterday was the old me. Today is The New Me! I see you coming, and I refuse to give in! I Am New! Anxiety is a thing of the past! The New Me is no longer anxious! I will conquer you! No more, no more, no more! Look at Me. Look at the New Me! I AM NEW!!!

What is this doing for you? You are focusing your mind, body, and soul on the fact that You Are New. You are now in control. Whatever the source of your anxiety is, it is no longer in control. You will need to practice this many times before it becomes second nature. Your belief will begin to grow as the results grow. You will begin to have confidence and optimism. You will have those moments when your heart begins to beat faster, and you begin to sweat. You may begin to feel disoriented. You remind yourself that You Are New. Using your Triggers, you begin to establish control. As you begin getting more proficient at using The RU NEW Principles, you will begin to establish better control of your anxiety. You are trying to establish control of the onset. In other words, if you cut it off at the pass, you have won the Battle! You see it coming. You strap on your armor! You exclaim, I Am New! You use your secret weapon, your triggers. You begin to calm down. You begin to establish confidence. You begin to realize you are in control. Eventually, you will overcome your anxiety.

There will always be moments with the potential for anxiety. You won't need to avoid people, places, or situations. You will begin living a fuller life. You won't be scared of moments that controlled you yesterday. Why? Because You Are New! You are In Control!

Welcome to The New You! You have conquered your anxiety! You are in control of you! Therefore, you are in control of the world

RU NEW?

around you. Your quality of life is getting better by the day. You are optimistic! Look at that big old smile on your face! Why is that smile so big?

Because............... YOU ARE NEW!!!!

CHAPTER 7

IT'S OVERWHELMING

ADDICTION

Addiction. When you hear the word, what immediately comes to mind? Is it someone that you know? Is it someone that you heard about? Or is it you? Regardless, if you are that somebody or know somebody, addiction is never to be taken lightly. An addiction consumes a person's life. Extreme addictions will control every aspect of your life. Because it has control, it has the strong possibility of ruining someone's life.

Most people have some type of addiction. For most, it's mild in nature and does not control their path. Some addictions are positive in nature. Think about it for a moment. Are you addicted to acceptance? Do you crave to be looked upon fairly? Are you consumed with your career? Do you find yourself having an uncontrollable urge to binge? Binge-watching TV? Something else mild in nature?

Today, in our society, mild addictions are not considered addictions at all. Maybe they're not. How you classify it is up to you. There are some addictions that cannot be denied. Food addictions. Drugs or Alcohol. There are others that are classified as serious. But any serious addiction has a severe negative impact on your life and those around you.

What have you done to kick your addiction? Have you gone to counseling? Or maybe rehab? Is there a reason that you haven't? Have you committed to seeking help only to make excuses why you shouldn't? Do you tell yourself that your problem is not serious? Are you worried about losing your job? Do you make up every excuse in the book to keep from seeking help?

RU NEW?

There comes a time when you have no choice but to seek help. What have you been doing so far? Has it worked? Are you still struggling even though you have been to counseling or rehab? It's time to try something New! The RU NEW Principles!

Why is addiction different from all other illnesses? Why do people abandon the addicted but will stand by their side through any other ailment? The common saying is "addiction is a choice ." But aren't some illnesses a product of choices? Eating and living choices? Physical health choices? These choices are still addictions.

Once the addiction really takes hold of you, you can no longer say it's a product of choice. Some say that if someone chooses to become addicted, then they can choose not to be addicted. Does that make any sense? Do you honestly believe that a person with a serious addiction has not made a choice to be free from addiction deep down in their soul? Addiction is not something that you can just flip a switch on or off at will. The struggle is turning it off!

The morality of supplying the habit. The struggle between the uncontrollable urge and the knowledge of the repercussions. Knowing that it may affect your job and your family. Though temporary, you will still pursue the satisfaction of supplying your addiction. It's a mental and physical struggle.

The majority of the battle is internal. Yes, there are tremendously beneficial external sources of help. By all means, you should pursue those external sources. But the serious battle is internal. The struggle with the guilt of yesterday. The feeling of inadequacy. The nauseating feeling that you get when you realize that you're disappointing your friends and family. The biggest part of the struggle is living in the past. Physically you are struggling in the present. Mentally you are fighting a fierce battle with the past.

So, let's fight the internal struggle. Everything yesterday is the old you. Today is New! The next moment in time is the New You! You must fight off the guilt and feelings of inadequacy. You must cleanse your body and soul. Now comes a moment of choice. You must choose to be New! You must remember the old saying, walking a mile starts with the first step. You may be saying that you have decided to end the addiction in the past, but you eventually regressed. First, let's work on getting our minds off of the addiction. Then, let's work at being the New You. Ask yourself, "Do I want to be New? Do you want to release yourself from this addiction? Of course, you do. No one wants to go through the pain and agony of addiction. No one wants to make their loved ones and friends suffer because of their addiction. So, you must become the New You!

How do you become New? You have determined that you want to be addiction free. The old you was addicted. But the New You will be free and live the life you want. That is New! That is the New You!

You will use internal and external triggers. Together, they are very powerful. The internal is focused on a couple of questions. Do I want to be New? Am I New? Concentrate! Ask the question, *RU NEW?* Do I want Control? Am I in Control? Yes, I am in Control? These are your internal triggers.

The external triggers are extremely important. We are visual and touch-sensitive creatures. Find something that is extremely valuable to you. A picture or a medallion. A piece of jewelry from someone that is very important to you.

RU NEW?

Regardless of what you choose, it needs to be significant to you. It is a very powerful weapon, your physical trigger, which will help you become the New You!

What is becoming New? Becoming New is being in control. Becoming New will give you the ability to fight off urges. The New You will not live in guilt and regret. Instead, being New will allow you to choose a path. A path to Recovery. A path of Control. A New path. A New You!

You must constantly ask yourself, *RU NEW?* Every reply is, Yes, I Am New! When that urge tries to overwhelm you, you must ask yourself, Am I New? Do not hesitate or waiver. You must shout audibly or internally; I Am New! What does that stand for? It stands for a stronger person. It stands for a person in control. It stands for a person that can conquer the addiction. The more you answer, I Am New, the more you will believe that You Are New. You will feel like your abilities are growing. Guess what? They are! Each moment that you practice being New, your ability to overcome your addiction will be stronger! You are beginning the transformation into the New You. And the New You will conquer the addiction!

Therapy and rehab are a struggle. Most programs are somewhat temporary. But the internal battle is permanent. No matter what you are struggling with in life, there will be an internal battle. Becoming the New Person that you need to be will be a struggle in the beginning. But the benefits of becoming New are countless. This will not happen overnight. We are all a work in progress. Being a New Person happens every day and every moment. Being New allows you to shed yourself of guilt and despair. The New You does not live in the past. You are no longer focusing on the failures of yesterday. You will stop saying that you can't.

RU NEW?

You will stop telling yourself that you cannot control your urges. That is a frame of mind that continuously drags you back into the pit of despair and regret. Living in the past will give you excuses for your actions today. Living in the past is the old you. Today, You Are New!

The New You is optimistic. The New You has hope. You have control. You are in control! What was in control yesterday is a figment of your imagination. When the urge hits, stand with pride and say I Am New! Stand strong and do not waiver. Keep repeating, I Am New, as many times as you need. Repeat it 100 times if that's what it takes. Repeat it until you believe it! Repeat it until the addiction believes it! The addiction is a Temporary Evil. It is a part of your past. The addiction is not a part of you! Because You Are New! You have control. It's your decision. And you know too well that your decision is to be Addiction Free! Replace the addiction with being NEW!

Being addiction free is easier said than done. I realize that. It may be a permanent struggle. But what are your choices? Do you choose to be addicted? Absolutely not! You need to have the weapons necessary to win every struggle. That struggle is internal. That is who you are. Who you are is a choice. But you have a Newfound Weapon. Along with rehab and therapy, you also have the powerful weapon called The RU NEW Principles! Your family and friends may not be therapists, but they surely can understand the Principles of Being New. And they can be a tremendous asset in helping you overcome your struggles. You are not alone! Let your people know that You Are New. Share your newfound weapon. Explain to them that their support is of the utmost importance. Ask them to help you by reminding you that You Are New. You are not alone.

There is that moment. You feel it trying to take over. You know what I'm talking about. That momentary uncontrollable urge. The anxiety. The disorientation. The nausea. The loss of reality. That uncontrollable urge to give in to the addiction. What do you do? The old you would give in. Am I right? Maybe you gave in periodically. Maybe it was once in a great while. The fact is, you gave into it. Plain and simple, this is an internal battleground! But that was yesterday. That was the old you. Now, You Are New!

There it is. The urge is welling up. In the past, you gave in. But today, You Are New. You remind yourself that You Are New. You ask yourself, *RU NEW?* I Am New! Yes, I Am New! I am In Control! At this moment, you use your external trigger. Let's say you have chosen a medallion that says I Am New. Hold the medallion or rub the medallion while you are repeating, I Am New. Continue this as long as you need to. At this point, the choices are simple. You continue practicing Being New and identifying yourself as a New Person. Or, you give in and revert back to the old you. The old addicted you. It is now a choice! You must draw the line in the sand! You are now in control! Because You Are New!

To become more powerful at being New, you must practice being New. When you wake up in the morning, find your trigger that says, I Am New. When you walk into the bathroom, there's a trigger on the mirror that says, *RU NEW?* Right below, it says, I AM NEW! Put them in a few places. Put them everywhere. Do what you need to do. The goal is to become New, which translates into overcoming your addiction. It doesn't stop at the moment you wake up. There are countless triggers in the outside world that will try to remind you of the old you. But you are mastering The Art of Being New! You will always have your *RU NEW Triggers.* You've decided on your chosen weapon! Keep the internal trigger primed and ready to go. Utilize it as much as possible. But don't forget your external triggers. The medallion or the jewelry, or whatever it is that you are using. Bring it with you everywhere you go. Without your internal and external triggers, anxious moments will cause you to revert back to the old you. Before today, those anxious moments were detrimental and had the advantage of control. But now that You Are New, armed with your *RU NEW Triggers*, you have the ability to overcome any anxious situation.

During bad days, you must constantly remind yourself *UR NEW!* On good days, you need to build your strength and your ability. Don't let your guard down. You are trying to attain Higher Levels of New. You are a work in progress. You are conquering your addiction! The New You has made its appearance in this world! Marvel at the moment! Rejoice and give thanks! You have conquered your addiction! You are now in Control. But do not let your guard down. The evilness of addiction will rear its ugly head periodically without you knowing it. Keep your armor strapped on! That New Armor that has changed your life! The armor called; *RU NEW!* In the past, when you were weak, it would use the frontal approach. But now that you are strong, it will try to sneak up behind you and attack when you are not expecting it. If you are not constantly practicing being New, you may revert back to your old ways. You must stand your ground. You must remain New!

RU NEW?

Your loved ones are a safety net. You have educated them in The RU NEW Principles. Hopefully, they are a part of the New Nation. Regardless, they are a safe zone. Your strongest moments will always be around those that you care about. Keep that in mind. Keep in mind that You Are New. You must constantly reinforce your Newness. Daily. Hourly. Moment by moment. Never stop asking yourself, *RU NEW?* And never stop shouting at the mountain tops; *I AM NEW!* Eventually, you will have to venture out of your safe zone. You will thrust yourself into the jungle of temptation. In the past, this has always been your true test. There will always be those people who will try to drag you down with temptation. They may not do it intentionally. But they still do it. Carry with you, always, your weapons to fight the temptations. Carry your *RU New Internal and External Triggers.* Use them as often as you must.

RU NEW?

Remember that each day forward should be a day that you are at a Higher Level of New! You will become stronger! You will develop Higher Levels of Control! The badge of power called *RU NEW* will grow stronger every day! You are the Conquering Hero!

Have you heard the term trading one addiction for another? Most of us have seen or experienced this firsthand. Trading tobacco for food. Trading alcohol for drugs. What *The RU NEW Principles* is doing for you is trading a negative addiction for a positive. A New Positive Addiction! You are creating New Positive Habits! You are creating an *RU NEW Addiction!* Your new habits will prevent guilt and the feelings of inadequacy. You are creating the habit of pride and self-control. Your thoughts are New thoughts. You have replaced the consuming thoughts of supplying your addiction with the powerful weapon of Being New! Every time you reflect on the past in a moment of weakness, you will have the powerful rebuttal of, I Am New! Your mind is becoming powerful! You are conquering the internal struggle! Today, you must master the art of Being New! You are replacing the thoughts from yesterday with your Newfound Powerful Weapon! You are trading negative thoughts for positive thoughts. You are trading the old you for the New You. You are trading the addiction for CONTROL!

Now that You Are New, you have a New outlook. What used to be an outlook of doom and gloom is now a vision of control and optimism. You have a renewed sense of pride and accomplishment. Your future has become bright. Each day you will understand how powerful you are becoming. How New you really are. Each day your outlook is a *Higher Level of New!*

RU NEW?

Venturing out can be a very trying event. There are many people, unknown to you, that are going to try you. When you are around people that you don't know, remaining New will take very little effort. But the true test is going to be your friends and some of your family. These individuals may have been a big factor in why you became addicted. They may be the bad influence that steered you into the addicted life. Have you heard the saying, you become the people that you associate with? How true this is. It takes a very strong person to overcome peer pressure. In most cases, we rely on our friends for advice. But some of these friends are bad news. They may be living the lifestyle that you were living. They may be the reason why you became addicted. Misery loves company. You know exactly what is meant by that comment. Can you remember the conversations you had with these individuals? They too were addicted.

RU NEW?

They were not interested in seeing you succeed in kicking your addiction. As a matter of fact, they may have been trying to hold you in that situation. Why? To say it plainly, you made them feel better knowing that they were not alone.

You may want to consider distancing yourself from these individuals for the time being. There are better choices that are supportive of your freedom from addiction. But don't forget about them. There will come a time when you are so strong at being New that you will be able to help them. You will show them how they can be New! Yesterday, you were someone who shared the same struggle. But now, You Are New! Now you are strong! Now you can be a mentor. You have sold out to Being New! You are now strong enough to withstand their temptations. You are capable of coaching them in *The RU NEW Principles*. You will be instrumental in eliminating their addiction. A glorious day will come when you look at them, and before you even ask the question, they shout, I Am New!

Being New applies to every aspect of your life. By practicing *The RU NEW Principles* as often as you possibly can, you will enhance all aspects of your life. And with that, you become far stronger in resisting the temptation of addiction.

Who are you? What are you? You are that individual that has conquered addiction! You are that person that has turned their life around! You are that individual who is Totally in Control! You are the perfect example for anyone who is struggling with addiction!

Wear it as a Badge of Courage. An example of Accomplishment. A role model for what it means to be New!

RU NEW?

RU NEW?

ABSOLUTELY!!

CHAPTER 8

DIGGING DEEP

PERFORMANCE

The necessity of physical performance. Have you had those days when you were physically not functioning properly? Those days when you are tired both physically and mentally? Days when you are just in a funk? Nothing seems to happen quickly. You are not functioning at your normal efficiency. We all have those days. That common saying; it's just one of those days!

One of those days? It is a test of your physical and mental fitness. There are choices that have to be made during moments like these. You can choose to fold up and lay down in the corner. Or you can use *The RU NEW Principles* to energize yourself. Your level of Newness and your belief in the Principles will allow you to function at a higher level. The old you may push through and accomplish some of your tasks somewhat efficiently. But using *The RU NEW Principles* will expand your ability to perform.

Performance is vital in all aspects of our life. In our relationships and our careers. In our financial decisions. Our parenting skills. Mental and physical health. Dealing with stress and anxiety. Your performance is of the utmost importance when dealing with addiction. Your performance today can and will determine your success and financial reward as a business owner. There is a list a mile long that is directly correlated to performance.

Fitness is of utmost importance for maximum performance. The mind is in a better place when the body is not struggling. Physical fitness will allow you to focus and perform at a higher level. When the focus of your attention is on the struggle due to your level of fitness, your focal point will be on that fact. The fact of you struggling. The fact that your performance is sub-par.

No matter what physical condition you are in, you can apply The RU NEW Principles to increase your level of fitness. Are you that person that only exerts themselves when needed? The person that is always trying to find a way out of any type of exertion? Are you the person that constantly doubts themselves? Do you understand where you can be? Have you wallowed out a hole in the couch due to a TV-watching marathon? You may be that person that will only accomplish the tasks that are of utmost importance. Or, you may be that person that is full of energy and is constantly striving to accomplish every task imaginable.

It does not matter who you are. It does not matter your level of physical and mental fitness. What was done yesterday was accomplished or not accomplished by the old you. Today you are using *The RU NEW Principles* to become that New productive person that performs at a higher level. Today, You Are New. Today you are in control. You must relinquish the mindset of the old you. It is time to become New. Living by yesterday's standards will offer every excuse in the book to not perform at a higher level. It is time to take that next step in performance. It is time to take over your mental and physical fitness. It is time to be New!

Methods of Physical Exertion. There are many forms of exertion. Exerting yourself has a different meaning for everyone. What takes a maximum amount of effort for one may be effortless for others. Everyone is at their own level. But it is vitally important to exert yourself no matter what level you are at presently. For some, there are certain tasks that require a maximum amount of focus. The same task, for others, may take very little thought. That does not matter. Today is a New Day. Today you are growing into that New Person that performs at a higher level.

Have you heard that saying, they are a natural? An example would be someone that performs at a high level during a physical activity such as Marathons or Iron Man competitions. It may be that person who is a beast in the gym. The person that works an eight-hour day and seems to perform at the same level every hour after. Maybe that person that has the garden of the month. What about people that always seem to have their act together? Everyone has something that they are capable of performing at a higher level. That is a phenomenal fact. It tells a person that they can perform at a higher level at any task they decide to take on. We all have that capability. But that capability is controlled by your mind. It is controlled by you. The old you will place doubt in your path. That is about to change because You Are New.

Are you like me, middle-aged and moving into those silver years? Can you remember back to the days when you had the ability to perform at a higher level without a tremendous amount of exertion? Your mind and body seemed to be programmed for maximum exertion without a whole lot of thought. Looking back, there were moments when you amazed yourself. It really didn't take much thought or effort to accomplish tasks. But those tasks today require more energy and desire to accomplish. As you begin to lose your physical fitness, your mind begins to take over. Your mind focuses on the fact that it's taking more effort to accomplish certain tasks. It's like quicksand. The more you focus on the fact that you're losing your physical abilities, the less likely you are going to put forth the effort to change your performance. We all suffer from this condition, just at different levels. There are periods of time in our lives when we just don't feel like doing anything at all. We know that we should. But we allow ourselves to make excuses. We decide not to put forth the effort to get our mind and body at a maximum level of performance.

You may have a physical condition that limits your ability to do certain things. But you have the ability to put forth what would be your maximum effort. No matter what your condition is or where your mental attitude has led you, you can put forth the effort to make changes in your performance life. You might be that person that is in peak physical condition. Also, You may be extremely strong mentally, but no matter what level you are at, there is always an opportunity for improvement.

Yes, you may have limitations physically, but mentally you have the ability to exert yourself and improve your condition. It is a struggle mentally. We all are guilty of convincing ourselves that we have certain limitations. Physically we do have limitations, but mentally there are no limitations. The limitations you have placed on yourself are based on the old you. It is the mindset of yesterday. It is what you have been telling yourself for many years. This causes stagnation in your growth. You must overcome this hurdle. You must shed the old you. You must ask yourself, *RU NEW?* Well, are you? The answer must be *YES, I AM NEW!*

By practicing *The RU NEW Principles*, you will learn how to exert yourself at a maximum level. You will not only exert yourself physically but mentally as well. The old you would say you can't. But the New You understands that the limitations that you've placed on yourself have been holding you back. As a result, the New You will grow stronger mentally, thus, overcoming the barriers that have been placed in front of you in days past. Let's look at some examples.

How about something as basic as housework or yard work? Yesterday, it was a struggle mentally. You told yourself how much you despised cleaning the house and straightening up the yard. You told yourself that it would be tiring both physically and mentally. You set the limitations for yourself before you even began the task. You may have struggled through it. But finishing the task in the old mental state has left a negative impact. The next time you are going to perform these tasks; you will have to overcome the same hurdle. But this time, the negative will be compounded. It's a double edge sword. It takes all that you have to accomplish the work. It's like quicksand, sucking you deeper into a negative frame of mind.

Maybe you are working overtime. You may be working in the heat or the cold. You may have a tyrant for a boss. It could be a negative situation being thrust upon you. It may be something as rewarding as playing with your children. It may be a workout at the gym. There are countless examples. It is that moment when you say; I don't want to do this. I'm tired, and my back hurts. I don't feel good, and my mind is toast. I'm aggravated and exhausted. I remember the agony of the task, and I am not looking forward to it. I am not looking forward to doing anything. Or, you're right in the middle of the task, and you begin to make excuses justifying why you should stop. This is the old you talking. You have excepted defeat before the game has even started. You have made yourself stagnant. And being stagnant causes regression.

But today, You Are New! You will refuse to let yesterday's attitudes and outcomes dictate your mindset for today. Today is a New Day. This is a New Task. This is a *NEW YOU!* You set no limitations. You have the ability to overcome exhaustion. You are now capable of putting forth that extra effort. All you have to do is remind yourself that You Are New! You are in Control!

Here is an example. There was a man that set a goal to run a mile and a half. Eventually, with the help of *The RU NEW Principles*, he was able to accomplish the goal. The reason for emphasizing *The RU NEW Principles* was due to the fact that he had been in a pretty severe car accident. Therefore, he had been sedentary for quite some time. He knew that he could use every excuse in the book to keep himself from accomplishing the goal. He knew that it would be a test physically and mentally. But he had been practicing The *RU NEW* Principles for quite some time. He applied them to his goal of running a mile and a half. Every time he hit the road, he had to struggle with doubt and physical condition. When his legs began to burn and his lungs were struggling for oxygen, the old person he was would try to defeat him. But he asked himself if he was going to allow the old person to dictate the outcome. Absolutely not, He reminded himself that He Was New. The burning sensation in his legs became a positive driving force. Because he was New, he realized that what he was feeling was maximum exertion. With maximum exertion comes increased physical condition. His lungs were burning and struggling for oxygen. His body was telling him that he needed to slow down. His mind was telling him to quit. The old person would quit. The New person pushed on. He had to continuously repeat to himself; I AM NEW! He had to tell himself I Am New to control his breathing. He would repeat I Am New over and over and over. And guess what? He eventually knocked out a mile and a half! He was overjoyed and had a tremendous sense of accomplishment. Oh, by the way, that man was me!

It was a tremendous moment! The old me would have been completely satisfied. But the New Me said, what's next? Yes, I was at a different level, both physically and mentally. But it was no time to stagnate. The old me would be convinced that I was incapable of higher achievements. You must set a new goal because You Are NEW! You have to push yourself! You must exert yourself by setting the bar a little higher!

I began carrying a stopwatch. My goal was to run the mile and a half one second quicker every time I ran. Yes, it was a struggle. There were days when I just didn't feel like getting out there and pushing myself. But I looked at myself in the mirror and asked a simple question, RU NEW? That question will give you a newfound energy. It will give you the right mindset. It will allow you to perform at a higher level.

RU NEW?

These principles apply to every aspect of your life. Everything that we do takes effort. And we constantly struggle with doubt. Doubt is old. But optimism is New! Bring your Newness to work. Bring it home. Bring it to the gym or the road. Bring the New You to the World.

The moment of exhaustion can be absolutely spiritual. The old you would be defeated. The New You puts a smile on your face, grits your teeth, and says I can accomplish this! You have a newfound energy because *UR New!* There are no limitations within you. Do not allow the old you and the people around you to dictate your accomplishments. You now have the ability to accomplish any task at a higher level. But you have to continuously practice being New. You must repeat to yourself that You Are New as often as you have to. Eventually, it becomes your culture. It becomes who you are. That moment of exhaustion is met with open arms. You understand that you are growing. You are becoming a Higher Level of New! You know that certain tasks will take maximum effort. Before, you looked at them with dread. Now you will begin craving the opportunity to push yourself. Why? Because *UR NEW!*

The Old Mindset. The old you. It will raise its ugly head periodically. It is to be expected. It is human nature. It is also societal. Those around you will be jealous of your accomplishments. They will try to fill your mind with doubt and defeat. This is just another test of being New. You need to expect it. You need to crave it. You need to understand that you are doing things right. Because you are New, others will be jealous and try to tear you down. It makes me excited! It should tell you that you have accomplished goals and dreams that others are not willing to perform at a maximum level to accomplish. This is the New You! It may be coworkers, or it may be family. It doesn't matter if it's your friends or your enemies. It is Fuel that will launch you into a *Higher Level of New!*

You will feel and see the difference every day from this point forward. When the old mindset kicks in, stand up tall. Grab your *Physical Trigger* and activate your *Mental Trigger*. Prove to yourself and the world that you are no longer old. You are the New and Exciting Person that you want to be! You are that person that is in control and can accomplish whatever you put your mind to! And use the old mindset as a benchmark. Use it as a standard to evaluate your level of Newness. See where you were and be excited about Where You are Going!

Honing in on the moment of exhaustion is now becoming exciting and almost euphoric. You are craving stressful and exhausting situations. It is compounding daily. Your Newness is making you stronger and more productive. Your

RU NEW?

Performance is increasing, and those around you are noticing. It will help you physically and mentally. It will reap huge benefits in your career or business. Your relationships will become stronger. You will see things with a different attitude. You will see a task that was troublesome in the past as being beneficial today. Every aspect of your life will become better. Your whole life is becoming *NEW!*

Your focus is New. You're not caught up in the minutia of yesterday. You're not allowing the old you to dictate anything in your life today. As your focus becomes more fine-tuned, you will be able to find different aspects of your life to apply *The RU NEW Principles*. It will be different for everyone. We all have certain aspects of our life that we struggle with. But by being New, we are able to identify each and every struggle in our life. Our focus has been on major tasks. But now that you are at a Higher

Level of New, you can begin fine-tuning the small aspects of your life. Your energy and power are tremendous. And it is growing by the day. You are becoming a Higher Level of New! Each and every step that you take, you are performing at a higher level than you could have ever imagined!

Your energy levels are soaring! You are becoming powerful! Your life is becoming an example for the power of *The RU NEW Principles.* You are knocking off one second on your mile and a-half run. You are becoming a better worker. A better business owner. A better partner. You are a *Better New Person!* Nothing and no one can stop you now! There are no limitations!

One more rep! One more mile! All your goals and dreams! You have reached a Higher Level of New. You are capable of going that extra step without doubt and limitations. You will be a locomotive going downhill! You will be unstoppable! But don't become complacent.

Becoming complacent will open the door for that old you to walk on through. The old you will struggle to overcome the New You. But it can happen. You must continuously practice *The RU NEW Principles* in every aspect of your life. Do not let your guard down. You must continuously remind yourself that *UR NEW* and you can accomplish anything that you perform at a higher level than most. You are attaining a Higher Level of New!

The Satisfaction of accomplishment is your weapon to combat complacency. Do not become cocky or arrogant. You must celebrate your accomplishments internally. That's where it counts. You must continue telling yourself that you can be at a Higher Level of New. You can perform at a higher level. You can accomplish more today than you did yesterday. Your power and energy are tremendous! Get off the couch and Go Get It! Go get it done! Go out into the world and become an example of being New!

Carrying it forward, what does that mean, carrying it forward? Your internal and external triggers are there to remind you that being New takes practice and determination. You no longer have the settle-for attitude. You are carrying it forward. You don't leave it at the house or in the car. You put it in your pocket or around your neck. You put it in your mind, and you make it part of who you are. You carry it forward by example. You are shouting to the world; I *AM NEW*! The energy that is created is infectious. Those around you will become more receptive and positive. By carrying it forward, your energy begins to be absorbed. Forgetting about The Principles will be detrimental to your growth. From this moment forward, every step you take should be the path to a Higher Level of New!

RU NEW?

The correlation between accomplishment and Performance is unbelievable. Yes, it doesn't take much of a brainiac to understand that you will accomplish good things if you perform well. But the correlation is far greater internally than it is externally. If you are in control, you are able to perform at a higher level. Therefore, you will accomplish far more than you can imagine. But most people will look at this correlation externally. They will say that you are lucky. Or you knew somebody. Or, you are that person that good things always fall in your lap without trying. Those people periodically increase their Performance. But internally, they are not growing. They are constantly doubting themselves. They're always throwing up excuses. Why they didn't accomplish, or they can't accomplish. The struggle is internal. Yes, there are external factors that may come into the scenario. But if you are strong internally, you are more capable of controlling the external factors. The old person will allow an external event to dictate the outcome of their life. They will expect something negative to happen. Expecting negative will make that individual focus on the negative. Yes, as soon as something that they perceive as negative arises, they will shut down. They are old. They live in the past. They allow yesterday to dictate the present. They are struggling internally. But they will not admit their faults. They are full of blame and envy. And that is not you. Why? Yes, *UR NEW!*

Because you have internal control, you are far more capable of handling external influence. You are a work in progress. You are growing every day. The external events are becoming less significant. Your Newness is coming to service in every aspect of your life. You are performing at a higher level. You are performing New!

RU NEW?

Increased Performance and higher levels of intensity will cause your accomplishments to compound exponentially. As your capabilities for higher intensity levels grow, Performance will increase significantly. Greater levels of Performance will transpire into greater accomplishments. You will have the ability to accomplish great things. Increased intensity for the Next Levels of New will become effortless. You will be leaving the old you behind forever. Why would you want to revert back to the old person that you were? Look at what you are accomplishing. Look at your Next Levels of New! Look at your enriched life! Understand what you used to be versus what you have become. This is a New Way of Life!

Admiration and opportunity will become more prevalent at each level of New. Be excited about the New Person that you have become. Seize the opportunities that will be put in front of you.

RU NEW?

Don't become complacent. There is a reason for increased opportunity. It is due to admiration. It is admiration from anyone that has seen your transformation into being The New You. Your boss will recognize your increased Performance and give you the necessary opportunities for advancement. The individuals that you were doing business with will base their decisions on your accomplishments and Performance. By being New, you will exude positive energy. That will transform into business opportunities. The admiration will flow over into every aspect of your life. Your relationships will be better. Your finances will be better. Your physical and mental health will be tremendous. It is all full circle. How did it start? You woke up this morning. You looked at yourself in the mirror; You asked yourself, *RU NEW?* And you shouted, *"I AM NEW!"*

RU NEW?

As you practice and perfect being New, you will become an example. A counselor, a mentor, or you may just have an awesome and fulfilling life. Those that are around you will see the benefits of being New. They will become curious. They may even become envious. One of the greatest accomplishments in this life is to enrich the life of another. So why would you want to hide *The RU NEW Principles* from those that are curious and envious? How much more enriched will your life be if they become New? If they utilize *The RU NEW Principles?* Living a New Life will be far easier when those around you are practicing the same New Life. As you perfect your skill, you will have people asking for your advice. You will become a coach or a mentor. You may be saying that you are not particularly excited about socializing with certain individuals. Yes, there are those individuals. And sometimes you have to deal with them on a daily basis. So why in the world wouldn't you share *The RU NEW Principles* with this dreaded individual? It may impact their life. It may change their life. They may become New. And guess what? They stop being a negative aspect of your life. Now they are someone that you can relate to. Now you don't mind socializing with that individual. You are becoming a coach!

People, I'm going to say it again. *The RU NEW Principles* have changed my life! It will change yours! But it will never change your life unless you begin practicing The RU NEW Principles. So what do you have to lose? A better question would be, what do you have to gain? Better Performance? Better physical and mental health? Better relationships? Better finances? How about just an enriched and happy life?

Do you want to be in control? Do you want to feel better? Do you want to accomplish more? Do you want to perform at a higher level? Then

RU NEW?

ask yourself the simple question RU NEW? And
your exuberant and excited reply is

I AM NEW!!!

CHAPTER 9

DO YOU BELIEVE?

FAITH

When you hear the word faith, what comes to mind? Is it what you believe? The conviction that something is true? Do you believe something so strongly that it has become your guide through the journey of life? Faith comes in many shapes and forms. We have faith in ourselves. We have faith in our loved ones. We have faith in a higher being. Or you may have faith that there is no higher being. No matter what form of faith we are talking about, it is the foundation of every aspect of our life. We will make major decisions based on our faith in what's right and wrong, what we were taught, what we have pondered, and what we have studied. Through others and the pursuit of knowledge, we establish our belief system, which is faith.

The power of faith is tremendously strong. History proves that. We have seen countries go to war over differences in faith. We have seen lives enhanced due to one's beliefs. We have also seen people's lives ruined due to differences in faith. Throughout history, faith has played a big part in shaping our world.

You may be that naïve individual that says you have no faith. How wrong you are. Some believe in a higher being, and others don't. If you believe that there is a higher being, you have faith. If you believe there is no higher being, you still have faith. The meaning of the word faith is usually tied to religion. A religion, a system of belief, or a lack thereof, are all forms of faith. It does not matter what your beliefs are; you have faith in something. The purpose of this chapter is not to legitimize a religion or a belief system.

RU NEW?

The purpose of this chapter is to point out the power of faith and how you can become stronger in your faith. Its purpose is to show you how to utilize *The RU NEW Principles* to become stronger in your faith.

Have you ever questioned your faith? If you are honest, the answer is yes. Why do I say that? If you did not question your faith, you would not ask questions. If you strongly believe in something, there will always be a doubt that creeps in. It is the way we learn. It's the way we become stronger in every aspect of our life. It's how we build conviction. It's how we build faith. By practicing The RU NEW Principles, your mind, body, and soul are open to knowledge. The old you may be content. You may not ask questions anymore. If you are not asking questions, you are not growing. Anything that you have faith in requires growth. That's how your faith gains strength. If you do not ask yourself *RU NEW*, you may become complacent. By practicing the art of being New, you automatically put yourself in a position of learning. The questions will be asked, and hopefully, they will be answered. Clarity comes from answered questions.

When you ask questions, who are you asking? Do you ask a person of knowledge? Let's hope you do. If you are asking the questions to a stagnant person or a person without knowledge, you are gaining nothing. In fact, it may be detrimental to your growth. Because You Are New, you are no longer apprehensive about asking questions. That is the old you. You are New! You are intimidated by no one! You are a sponge sucking up as much knowledge as you possibly can! This all works hand-in-hand with every subject that we have talked about so far. You are a New Person. The old you is not in control. The pursuit of knowledge is the pursuit of power. The pursuit of power, or should we say strength, will put you at a *Higher Level of New* every single moment of your life!

There are times that we do not rely on another individual to seek knowledge. Sometimes we rely on the powers around us and in us. Some may use meditation. Others chant. Some use prayer. And others use deep internal thinking. You may be that individual that says there is no external or internal power. Well, let's think about that. Do you go throughout your entire life without a single thought or feeling? You know the answer to that. Do you come across a situation that requires deep thought? Once the thought process begins, do you feel your energy or mood begin to change? It may be positive or negative. It may be pleasant or painful. Regardless of your internal response, you are gaining knowledge from internal power. You may say that it's an animal response. OK! Does that internal reaction give you knowledge? Is there not an internal power present? If your answer is still no, then the point is proven. The fact that you believe or you don't believe is faith. You have faith in your belief. Regardless of what you believe or don't believe, you must constantly increase your knowledge and ability to have conviction in your faith.

A few years back, I conversed with an individual I've known most of my life. We were comfortable with discussing practically anything. At the time, this person was a devout Christian. They only believed in the power of prayer. During our discussion, I mentioned that I was intrigued with meditation. You could swear that I had slapped them in the face. They were appalled. They began showing me the power of their faith. The discussion continued. The question was asked, how did you come to such a strong conviction about your faith? Their answer was knowledge. With knowledge from individuals that were considered to be an expert, I posed an additional question. Although you have a strong knowledge of your faith along with a powerful conviction, have you ever pondered the idea of gaining knowledge of other people's differences in faith? Would that make you even stronger? They pondered the question and struggled with it for a moment. Then they replied, yes.

We are close till today. But today, this individual, this friend, stated that being open to others and their faith has made them stronger in their own personal beliefs. The reason for this personal reflection is to emphasize the point of seeking knowledge, of being New. Practicing *The RU NEW Principles*. By being NEW, you will ask questions. You are seeking knowledge. Your faith and beliefs may not change, but they will become tremendously stronger. We can gain knowledge from anyone at any time. Understanding and appreciating an opposing thought only makes you stronger. But you have to have a New Attitude. You have to quit being bullheaded. It is time to ask yourself the question once again. *RU NEW?*

By becoming New, you're increasing your ability to acquire knowledge. By acquiring knowledge, you're building faith. First, you must shed the old you. You must relinquish your old habits. You must build your arsenal for acquiring knowledge. Also, you must be open and receptive to other people's beliefs. There must be respect. If you want someone to respect your beliefs or faith, you must first be open to learning their viewpoint.

Because you are practicing *The RU NEW Principles*, I am challenging you. I challenge you to grow as a New person and open your mind to other people's beliefs. I am not saying to change your faith. What I am challenging you to do is to grow more powerful in your faith. Take the time to listen and ponder another person's beliefs. When it's all said and done, you will find that there are similarities in everyone's belief system. By understanding this, you become extremely powerful. Your faith will grow stronger!

Once you have increased your knowledge and acceptance and grown more powerful in your faith, you are now prepared to show it in your actions. It does not matter what you have faith in. It is the fact that you have become more powerful in your faith. It could be your beliefs spiritually, or it could be your faith in your loved ones or your coworkers. But, it is definitely faith in yourself! You are now ready to co-mingle your faith with your actions.

Have you had those moments where you felt so strongly about something that it was completely evident in your words and actions? That was due to faith. A strong, powerful faith in whatever it is that you believe will become extremely evident in your actions. The increase in knowledge transforms into belief. Belief becomes faith. Faith becomes power. That power becomes evident in your actions. Example, you start a new job. You do not know much about the tasks that you are required to conduct. Because you are unknowingly practicing *The RU NEW Principles*, you are highly receptive to learning at a higher rate. You showed up to work at a *Higher Level of New* every single day. As a New employee, you are more receptive to gaining knowledge. The rapid increase in knowledge gives you confidence. With that confidence, you become more proficient. Proficiency produces performance. The performance turns into power. That power turns into faith. Somewhere in this journey when faith kicks in, your actions convince others of your faith in yourself and in your ability to accomplish the task. Do you see the correlation between faith and performance?

You are with a group of friends that you have known most of your life. All are comfortable with any subject of discussion. Inevitably someone will bring up their spiritual beliefs. For this example, we will say that there are vast differences between everyone in the discussion. The old you would lock your heels in. You would argue until you were blue in the face about your beliefs. You argue that your belief is the only correct belief. You may become angered and aggravated. The discussion may become heated. The heated discussion may cause animosity.

That was the old you. Today you are New. You are more tolerable and receptive. You are open to gaining knowledge of another person's beliefs. Now you are becoming more tolerant of a discussion such as this. You are now becoming more powerful because you are gaining knowledge. You're not suffering from a mental block. You are not locking your heels in. Because your beliefs are now becoming evident in your actions, others will begin to become curious to know more about your beliefs. You are both receptive at this point. You're open to gaining knowledge. You may not detract from your faith, but understanding someone else's faith will make you far stronger.

This does not only apply to spiritual faith; it applies to every aspect of your life. Your faith is tested every single moment. Your faith in yourself and others. Your faith in your ability to control a situation or how to react in other situations. How can you have confidence in your faith or belief if you have never been open to an idea or action? I will say it again. Power comes from faith, and faith comes from knowledge. By being New, you will become extremely receptive to gaining knowledge.

Staying strong in your beliefs during trying moments becomes less of an effort once you start attaining Higher Levels of New. The testing of your faith will be less stressful. You will have more confidence. Your faith is growing stronger by the day. But, as in every scenario, there is the possibility of complacency. That is why you must continue practicing *The RU NEW Principles*. Don't forget your External and Internal Triggers. Use them as much as you possibly can. It will only make you stronger. Eventually, this will become your culture. The positive results will emphasize your belief in The RU NEW Principles. The New You will refuse to become complacent. Why? If things are this good today, why wouldn't you want him to be better tomorrow?

RU NEW?

You may be that individual that is filled with self-confidence. Or you may struggle with confidence. You can always improve your self-confidence no matter where you fall in this spectrum. Self-confidence is an aspect of faith. Why? As you build your self-confidence, you will begin to exert more action. By making an effort to acquire the knowledge, you will begin to build self-confidence. As your self-confidence grows, so does your faith in yourself. You will no longer doubt yourself in certain situations. It does not matter where you fall in the self-confidence realm, faith in yourself will increase if you continuously practice *The RU NEW Principles.*

You have arrived! You have found an exhilarating surge of faith. Your self-confidence is climbing. All of the aspects of your life are changing. You're becoming a better person. You are becoming a New Person! Now you will begin

RU NEW?

using *The RU NEW Principles* to be tolerable, understanding, and optimistic.

Your abundance of self-confidence will make you more tolerable. Tolerable of others. Others will be more tolerable of you. But most of all, you will be far more tolerable of yourself. Tolerance is a sign of contentment in one's self. The internal struggle to justify one's actions becomes nonexistent. Plain and simple, you have extreme faith in yourself. The fact that you have faith in yourself will allow you to be more tolerable of others. Your focus is no longer on yourself. It gives you the leeway to understand what other people are dealing with. Your tolerance will be vast. You will be more understanding of your coworkers and understanding of your family and loved ones. And yes, you will be far more tolerable of those wild and unruly kiddos. Your tolerance of yourself will allow you to focus your energies on more important situations.

With tolerance, there is a newfound understanding. You begin to see things in yourself and others that you did not see before. You begin to understand why you and others do certain things in certain situations. Because your eyes are open, you will understand. It does not matter if your understanding brings you to the conclusion that the actions of an individual are negative or positive. It allows you to understand the complexity of every single individual. Good people have bad days, and bad people have good days. Your understanding will give you the ability to distinguish whether their actions are a moment in time or it's just who they are. A higher level of understanding will increase your tolerance. And your tolerance will give way to optimism.

RU NEW?

Being optimistic will allow you to see the bigger picture. Your optimism will give you the ability to search for the positive in every moment. But it will also give you the understanding that the negative is just a part of life. Therefore, it is extremely important to be optimistic in negative situations. Optimism in those moments comes from faith in yourself, Faith in your ability to overcome. Faith in your ability to be optimistic no matter what the situation is.

Where does this new faith come from? It began when you started your journey practicing *The RU NEW Principles*. And what a journey it has been! Your growth has made positive changes in every aspect of your life. Your faith is deeply rooted. Faith comes from believing. It also comes from conviction. Conviction comes with experience. Unless you are practicing *The RU NEW Principles*, you will never see the conviction of your faith at its highest level.

RU NEW?

A huge benefit of being New is knowing that everyone has their own version of faith. Because you are New, you are now open to learning their viewpoint and the reason for their faith. As your level of New increases, your tolerance and understanding will be greater. You are becoming a complete person. You are a New Person. But don't become complacent. There is a *Higher Level of New* every single day. Keep practicing and mastering *The Art of Being New*.

As you continue your journey, your growth and strength will attract others who are seeking a better life. As you attain a *Higher Level of New*, your energy will be so strong that it is unavoidable for most people. You will become an example of New, and you will influence their life. They will be curious about your positive changes and strengthening faith. Unknowingly, you will become their guide; their guide to *The RU NEW Principles*. In every social encounter, you will have the opportunity to share your New strength and faith. Do not pass up the opportunity to bless someone with the skills to better their life. Become the example. Become the teacher. Living New will be the opportunity. Living your life New will be the example. Your strengthening faith and confidence will give you the desire to share your faith and how *The RU NEW Principles* have enhanced your life. If being New benefits only one other person in this world, you have accomplished a goal that very few individuals have experienced!

Do not forget how you became New. Do not get complacent. Always go back to your roots. Utilize your internal and external triggers in every moment and situation of your daily life. Always remind yourself that You Are New. Start every day as a New Day and an opportunity to attain a *Higher Level of New*. Take your first steps of the day as a New Person.

RU NEW?

Always be excited about the opportunity for growth. Use every opportunity to practice *The RU NEW Principles*. By doing this daily, you will attain a Constant Higher Level of New. Understand that *The RU New Journey* will strengthen your faith in yourself. Your faith in your abilities to conquer any challenge. The faith that your constant increase in strength will have no limits as long as you continue your RU New Journey. Never stop absorbing the energy of your external triggers. We are so responsive to our senses. The touch of your triggers. The feeling of power. The faith in yourself when you see that sticky note that exclaims, "I Am New!" The exhilaration of knowing that you can conquer the world. The constant growth of your internal power. Your internal triggers are a weapon to overcome any obstacle. You are becoming the Newest Person on Earth! I cannot emphasize enough that you must continue using your triggers. *The RU New Triggers* are the root cause of your Wonderful New Life.

The inner circle. That ever-growing inner circle. Your faith will grow exponentially as you become surrounded by individuals that are taking the same *RU NEW Journey*. The constant growth of your inner circle will increase your power. Your feeling of self-worth and accomplishment will be emphasized by the circle of people walking the same path. Being New and sharing *The RU NEW Principles* will comfort you because you are a positive influence in their lives. You are responsible for building the RU NEW Nation! If you have made a positive change in just one person's life with The RU NEW Principles, then all you have done to become New was worth it. You will have a feeling of self-worth, a feeling of accomplishment; that wonderful feeling of knowing that you have changed somebody's life by being an example and sharing The RU NEW Principles.

There is power in numbers. As the numbers grow, so will your faith. What will your world be like if you are surrounded by people that have faith and are practicing *The RU NEW Principles?* That's a no-brainer. So why wouldn't you share? You could continue being surrounded by negative stagnant people, or you can enhance your life by building your inner circle. Build the *RU NEW Nation!* Successful people are empowered by surrounding themselves with people of a like mind. So, I ask, why would you not share this with everyone in your life? You will also thrive and grow if you help them build their New Life. Share by your actions. When they are in a bad situation, ask them, *RU NEW?* Be their support system because there may come a time when you will need their support. So, if you are enhancing their New Life,

RU NEW?

their new growth will be beneficial in your time of need. Build your world. Your *RU NEW World!* You may be heard if you are alone shouting, "I Am New!". But, if your inner circle is standing together and shouting "WE ARE NEW," the world will hear you!

Apply *The RU NEW Principles* to every aspect of your life. Share them with anyone that is receptive. Have faith in your New Turbo-Charged Way of Life. You will create a New World. *The RU NEW NATION!*

So I ask.......

RU NEW? Do you have faith?

Take the *RU NEW Journey* and reply......

I AM NEW!!!!!!!

CHAPTER 10

THE RUG RATS

CHILDREN

Rugrats, kiddos, my little blessings, or mini-me. The next version of you, just in a smaller size. Children are the most wonderful gifts of life. They are capable of showing us what New is all about. Raising children can be a challenge. There are those moments they put this huge smile on your face. Then there are those moments where you want to pull your hair out and scream. But this exercise in raising children is more beneficial than you ever imagined. If you allow it to, it will teach you so many things about yourself and how you view the world. Children, the New version of you, are more receptive today than they will ever be in their life.

RU NEW?

There are so many books and articles that give us advice on how to raise children. Some have the soft psychological approach. Others have the iron fist approach. Some have you using rewards and penalties. But none that I have read, although there may be a few, have focused on the awesome inner power of a child. None show you the technique to allow your child to release that power. In other words, you will show your child how being New and using *The RU NEW Principles* will allow them the ability to conquer the world without stress and anxiety. *The RU NEW Principles* will allow your child to grow without having to depend on external stimulation to find inner peace. There is no perfect "How to" book on raising children. Each and every child is different. Therefore, the best technique to raise a child will vary from child to child. However, there is one common denominator with every child. They all come into this world New. They all start the unbelievable path of education and experience at the moment of birth. *The RU NEW Principles* are already in place. It's your job to show them how to use it.

Bringing children into the world is a huge commitment, whether planned or unplanned. If they're planned, you have definitely committed. If they were unplanned, it's time to get committed. There is a little person that needs you and will rely on you to be their guide. If that job does not become your priority, the one that suffers the most is the child. But don't make the mistake if you lack commitment; you will also pay the price.

Reflect back to your childhood, if you can. Do you remember thinking to yourself, why on earth do my parents continuously say and do certain things? They sound and act old. Then, later on in life, you begin to understand why certain things were said and done. Before long, you begin acting like them and sounding like them. You ask yourself, "why didn't I listen to them in the first place?" Well, it's called the learning process. We have certain traits and thoughts that we were born with. One that we are definitely born with is being New. Throughout our upbringing, we practice The RU NEW Principles without ever having heard of them. Somehow, someway, we lose sight of being New. Well, that's about to change. It will change for you and your child.

For newborns and toddlers, it is critical that you practice being New. They don't need the practice because they are New. They just don't know it. This is the most receptive time in their life. They are New to every opportunity and experience. They are a sponge for learning. Their knowledge is sculpted during the early years. Under normal circumstances, you are the example. So, you better get busy being New. As you well know, your attitude will turn into theirs. Your old way of thinking will sculpt them into being an old-minded person. You should never approach your newborn or toddler as an old thinking person. You must be New. You must practice *The RU New Principles*.

Starting them in this world using *The RU NEW Principles* is the greatest gift you will ever give them. If you are about to have a child or you have a newborn or toddler, now is the time to begin the journey of being New. You will learn and grow together. You will become New as One. Go Team New! Together you will become an unstoppable force. We all want the best for our children, correct? So why not teach them how to be the most stable and powerful person they can possibly be?

Be an example for them. Be New for them. When you allow stress and anxiety to control you, they see this. When they see you having trouble getting your act together, they begin to believe that is normal. If you are not practicing *The RU NEW Principles*, then you are giving them the old you as an example. They learn from what they see and hear. They feed off of your energy. If you are unstable, they will be unstable. The same is true for stress, anxiety, anger, and pessimism. Remember, they are a New Version of You. What you are, they will become. If you're allowing yesterday to control you, you are setting a terrible example. Yesterday is what you've learned. It is not today or tomorrow. Learn from your experience, but by all means, you must be New today. Do you want your children to be well-adjusted and self-confident? Do you want them moving forward or standing still, gazing behind them? We all want what's best for our children. So, let's be the most positive and influential person in their life.

RU NEW?

What they see as New, they will become. For the sake of that little person, you must constantly ask yourself RU NEW. You must have belief. Faith that You Are New. Guess what? If you are not new, chances are you are setting your child up to be the old you. No matter how good the old you was, the New You is a better version. And that better version is what you want for your children, correct?

Toddlers are definitely a challenge. Some are more challenging than others. They are a bundle of energy and curiosity. Now that's a huge lesson in being New. They are New and have no idea what being New is. Did you ever think that you could learn from your toddler? Well, guess what? Now is a learning moment. Being New as an adult will have you striving for positive energy. Being New will give you an open mind. Therein lies curiosity. Do you understand that we all started New? We look at this little bundle of joy with amazement. We are totally amazed at the amount of energy within that little human being. I don't know about you, but I have commented many times that I wish I had the energy of that toddler. While their curiosity can be a test of your patience, you should look at their example and strive for that quest for knowledge.

Curiosity should be encouraged. Yes, there are some limitations. But, within the boundaries of their safety, you should allow them to explore life with all the intensity they can muster. Remember, they are New. As you get to *Higher Levels of New* personally, you will understand and encourage their journey in this New World.

"But they won't listen!" They were told 20 times, and they seem to be ignoring you. The old you would look at this as rebellion. By being New, you are open-minded and tolerant. Understand that it is not rebellion but the search for identity.

218

RU NEW?

You may see aggression or passivity. No matter the toddler's temperament, you must be receptive and realize that their personality is coming forward. With their personality coming forward, you have a huge opportunity for growth. Yes, they are a smaller version of you. They are unique and one-of-a-kind. By being New, you will strive to grow with them instead of creating roadblocks to mold them into your personality. You are encouraging curiosity and the pursuit of knowledge. Start them early in life with *The RU NEW Principles*. Let the principles become ingrained in them as they grow into the unique person they were meant to be.

Then they're off to school. Hopefully, you have encouraged the pursuit of knowledge, self-discipline, and morality. In the early school years, they are challenged with required schoolwork and personal conduct guidelines. If your young person is struggling with who they are and who they can become, they will have focus issues. You are showing them how to remain focused by encouraging them to remain new. They will understand that being New will instill an unquenchable desire for knowledge and growth. What they learned yesterday will vault them into a *Higher Level of New*. Today they are New, and their passion is strong. A higher level of New equates into a higher level of knowledge. A higher level of self-confidence. You should always emphasize the benefits of being New. Today is a brand New day and an opportunity to become smarter and a better person. You will be making your child into a very powerful human being. They will succeed no matter what they decide to venture into.

Dealing with social issues and peer pressure is a challenge that most children will face. If you are actively being a part of your child's life, they will not have to deal with it alone. This is definitely a moment that both of you need to be New. You will launch yourself into the protective mode. Rightfully so. We definitely want to protect and shield our children. However, if the old you prevail, you will meet the situation with aggression and denial. You may give your child advice based on the old you. The old you may not be tolerant and understanding. The old you may not see the big picture. In this situation, by being New, you will clearly understand how peer pressure is a learning moment.

The old you may use a comment like, "if your friends jumped off a cliff, would you jump off of the same cliff?" While jumping off a cliff is definitely not a good idea, it really does not address the root cause of the problem. The problem is not jumping off a cliff. The real problem is why would they do it. By teaching them to be New, they will determine that their peers are not thinking straight and looking at the big picture. By them being New, they will be far more analytical. They will be stronger and less likely to succumb to peer pressure. They will think for themselves. They will not make decisions based on the mounting pressure from days past. They will have an understanding that they are stronger today than yesterday. The old way of thinking gives way to weakness. They have a desire for identity and acceptance. If you are teaching them the RU New Principles, they will be self-confident. They will know that they are a unique individual, an individual that thinks for themselves. They are in control. Not their misguided friends. They will stand tall and wear their badge of courage of being New.

With this weapon of being New, they will have a stronger desire to be more attentive because they are craving knowledge. They will be more disciplined because they are full of self-confidence. They no longer need to act like a clown for attention. Because you are walking the walk, they will respect you more. By being the example and the positive impact of being New, they will be more self-adjusted. Both of you will have less stress and anxiety. Life is good! Life is New!!

Then they become Teenagers. Hopefully, your household is living by *The Principles of Being New*. Teenage years are a whole new set of issues. The exposure is increased. The temptations are stronger. The expectation of adulthood magnifies the search for identity. Some will become an instant genius. Some will become natural-born leaders. Some will be comfortable with being a follower. Others will struggle with academics and social life. They may become a recluse. But, on the other hand, they could blossom in unexpected avenues. The teenage years are a test for both of you. There are many transitions. It does not matter where your teenager is at this moment. They will be more self-confident and ambitious in the days to come due to *The RU New Principles*.

The struggles are real. It is called life. For most, they take it as it comes. They deal with it the best that they can. For the majority of society, it is a journey of successes and failures, ups and downs, and moments of happiness or despair. The issue for most is there is no plan. There is no system. There are no principles until now. Taking things as they come when dealing with issues is a noble thought. If your teenager does not know how to deal with issues correctly, you are allowing others in their world to dictate their outcome.

So, it's time to take a stand. A stand for you and your child. It is time to practice the principles to deal with it. It is time to be New! Starting with you, you must live as a New Person. You must be the example. Your teen needs your guidance.

RU NEW?

Your guidance is your actions. Your example is living *The RU New Principles*. What is it to be New? Being New is living today. Today is a new day. It does not matter what happened yesterday. You cannot live in or change the past. You must look at every situation as an opportunity for growth, no matter how serious the situation is. Living New allows you to perform at higher levels. It allows you to have a stronger faith in yourself and others. Being New will make you understanding, tolerable, excepting, and very strong. There are many aspects of the teen years that are very joyful. There are some that are very trying and can be life-changing. How situations are handled will determine whether the changes are positive or negative. You owe it to your teen to live New and to teach them *The RU New Principles*. Teach by example because there will come a time that they will be tested. And at that moment, you will be judged based on your actions or lack thereof.

Let's touch on some of these serious situations. If you open your eyes, you will see that anxiety is running rampant through society. Whether you agree that anxiety is real, your teenager more than likely does. As in the previous chapters, it has been pointed out that anxiety is life-changing. Anxiety can consume their entire life. They will live in fear of the stressful situations that cause their anxiety. Whether you believe it to be true or not, it is still something that they have to deal with. It will affect their attitude. It will affect their education and social well-being. In some instances, it will affect their entire life. Social situations and peer pressure can cause severe anxiety. Not knowing how to deal with the anxiety can thrust them into panic attacks. Panic attacks will give way to bad decision-making. The decisions will be made based on trying to appease the anxiety. Their focus will be on their anxiety, not the method to eliminate it. The old you will tell them to suck it up and deal with it. Some will go as far as telling their teen that they're imagining things. It may not seem real to you, but it is real to them. Reality is in the results. You must acknowledge that as reality, if the results are bad grades, rebellion, or a generally poor attitude. If they think all their problems are caused by anxiety, then yes, it is real. It is real to them.

So, what do you do? Anxiety is driven by yesterday. It is driven by examples. It is based on the actions or reactions to stressful situations yesterday. It gets imprinted into their brain. That situation is now a trigger. They are expecting it to cause anxiety anytime the same moment occurs. So, what do you do? What do they do? You must teach, and they must learn how to be New. How do you understand that today is a New Day? They need to realize that the events that have caused their anxiety in the past should not dictate their actions and reactions today. By being New, they understand what triggered the anxiety yesterday. By being New, they are receptive and tolerant. They have to establish control. Control of themselves and the situation around them. They now understand what causes their anxiety. That is a huge step in a positive direction. Identifying the situation or the moment is half the battle. Most that suffer from anxiety never really hone in on the source of the anxiety. By understanding the trigger, they can now get prepared to fight back. Teach them to replace the anxiety triggers with *The RU New Triggers*. Teach them to use their Newfound Principles as a tool. A tool to stop the onset of anxiety. They must understand that they are New. Understand that they're in control. Understand and believe that they will no longer suffer from anxiety attacks. A medallion, a sticky note, a rock, or whatever they choose can be the physical trigger that establishes control at the onset of an anxious situation. They can now control their anxiety because They are New!

What is your part? This is your child. You know them better than anyone else on this earth. You can see the change in your child without a whole lot of effort. You have learned the signs of the onset of an anxiety attack. Your part in the scenario is not only to teach them *The RU New Principles* but to live them as well. Sharing with them what causes your anxiety will be extremely beneficial. You may say that you do not have anxiety. I beg to differ. Every human being suffers from some level of anxiety. You just need to sit down and ponder. Search your soul to identify what those situations are. Then you can correlate the anxious moment and your practice of being New. Share with them. Make them understand that they are not alone. Let them know that everyone experiences anxiety. And by all means, you must emphasize that it can be controlled. Controlled by being New! When you see the onset, tell them to remember They Are New. Ask them *RU NEW?* Continue asking them if They Are New. Do you want to stop your anxiety? Then use your Triggers and remind yourself that You Are New. You are in control! You are *NEW!*

Depression is another condition that is prevalent during the teenage years. In some cases, it may start before their teens. Depression is a very serious condition. Depression can absolutely wreck a life. It can also wreck lives around them. In extreme instances, it can result in suicide. This I know from personal experiences. Depression is a silent killer. Left unchecked, it begins to consume an individual. Without help, it may be disastrous. Depression in teens can be identified. You know your child. You can see the changes in them. Do not have a blind eye. Analyze them. Ask them questions. Do your best to determine what is the cause of their change in attitude and mood.

There are medical professionals that specialize in depression. I strongly encourage you to seek their help. Seek counseling as soon as possible. But you must remember that the doctor or counselor cannot be with them 100% of the time. Neither can you. You need to arm them with a weapon to combat depression. That is *The RU NEW Principles.*

Depression is a product of negative energy. All you have to do is look for the signs to come to that conclusion. A lack of motivation. A feeling of no self-worth. A life filled with pessimism. You can see it in their demeanor. They are moving slower. Their attitude is negative. Their outlook on life has changed. And that outlook is not very promising. Depression is a progressive condition. The symptoms will progressively get worse if not addressed.

Whether you want to believe it is true or not, you must conclude that the condition is real. You must act immediately. You must shut off the flow of negative energy. Instead, fill their lives with hope, optimism, and positive energy. I hope that you have sought medical help or counseling. But you must address the issues outside of that realm. It is time to begin pumping positive energy into your child. It is time to implement *The RU New Principals.*

Teaching them to be New will begin to shift the focus away from yesterday. Yesterday was filled with negative. Not much optimism or hope. The old person would dwell on days past. All of the negative aspects of those days. But today is New. They are New. It is time to reverse the tide of negative. Being New; it gives them hope for today. They begin to be optimistic. They begin to establish self-control. How do they do that? They must use *The RU NEW Triggers.* You must put them in their hands. You must teach them how to use them. Using the Visual Triggers at the start of every day will be the first step in a positive direction. They will understand that they have a weapon to combat their depression. They understand that this is a New Day. They are in control! They have come to the realization that they are suffering from depression. Now it's time to identify the onset of a depressed state. By using their *RU NEW Trigger*, they must understand that they are their defense when the onset of depression begins. Internally they must constantly remind themselves that They Are New. They must relentlessly ask themselves, RU NEW? As they begin to see the positive results of living as a New Person, their faith in themselves and their self-worth will begin to grow. This is the injection of positive energy. These are the steps to recovery. It must be constant. It must become a Way of Life. It must become who they are. And, who are they? *THEY ARE NEW!*

When your child begins to see the benefits of *The RU NEW Principles,* they will begin to believe. Most of all, they will begin to believe in themselves. Their strength will begin to grow. Their opinion of themselves will be positive. This will translate into better relationships and higher success in their education. Their relationship with you will begin to transform into something that we all want. The benefits are endless. There is no reason to believe that *The RU NEW Principles* will not positively impact both of you. Self-worth and optimism will combat anxiety and depression. It will overcome addiction. It will improve relationships. It will make them a better person. It will make them a New Person.

You must build your teen's faith in The RU New Principles. But first, they must have faith in you. For your teen to have faith in you, you must have faith in yourself. As the old saying says, you must walk the walk. They will believe if you believe. Therefore, you must begin practicing *The RU New Principles* today. Every day that you don't is one less day of your teen's peace and tranquility. Today is the best day to start if you have not started practicing The RU New Principles. Then, you and your teenager can start the journey together. You will share in the triumphs. You will both see amazing growth and an all-around better life. You both will be equipped to handle any situation that is thrown in front of you. *Y'ALL ARE NEW!*

As both of you are taking this wonderful journey together, your relationship will get better by the day. You will begin to see the positive results right away. The communication will be open. The confidence in each other will grow. You will be their support system. But now comes the test. Dealing with their relationships outside of the home. Most individuals in their life, more than likely, are not practicing *The RU NEW Principles.* But that can change. You must encourage them to find someone that is going down the same path as they are—emphasizing the art of being New and looking for someone that will share their outlook on life. Some of their relationships and interactions may be the root cause of their problems. As they begin to grow, they will begin to identify and understand who is a contributing factor and why. That individual will have a choice to make. They will be curious and begin to ask questions. As they ask questions and see the changes in their life, they will then have a desire to pursue living a

New Life. Or they will be intimidated because of being shallow-minded and eventually disappear from your teen's life. Either way, they win. As they begin to grow, their friends will ask questions. This will be their opportunity to share *The RU NEW Principles*. And that is definitely a win. Like-minded people travel in the same direction.

You may deal with some rebellion. Give it time they will grow. They will begin to understand. Then, they will become New. Encourage them to use *The RU NEW Principles*. Do not beat them in the head with it. That will only compound the issues. You need to be the example. You need to show them the benefits of being New. You must practice the principles so that they can see the benefit. They will come around. Just be patient and diligent. Never give up. Why? Who else do they have? Believe it or not, you are the biggest influence in their life. If you feed them negative and bad examples, you will continue to see their issues grow. Be positive. Be the example. Be New!

With that said, you need to realize that the External Trigger could be you.

You may be that one bright point in their life that they rely on when they are in bad situations. Be an active part of their transformation and their life. Let them know that they can always rely on you. First, you must ask yourself the question. Am I living my life as a New Person? Am I the example that they need to rely on? They must have faith that you are their cornerstone if you want them to rely on you. Giving empty advice and living a poor example will only compound their issues. Practice being New. Live New!

When they call, and you realize that they're in a bad situation, you must first ask yourself, Am I

RU NEW?

Thinking New? If you're going to teach them and advise them that they are New, you must first be New yourself. Believe me, they will know. Put yourself in their situation. Be understanding and tolerant. Have an open mind and be prepared to hear the truth. That is what you're looking for, correct? The truth? No matter how concerning the truth is, both of you are one step closer to overcoming whatever issue it is that they are battling. You are succeeding! But most of all so is your teenager!

Understand who your teenager is. Understand what their interests are. Try your best to take an interest in what they are interested in. Why? Because you are trying to create as many communication avenues as possible. They may be consumed in the world of texting. Social media may be their main avenue of communication. Very few use the intended purpose of a cell phone. Right "RU NEW?" on a sticky note and put it on their mirror. Write a note of encouragement and put it in an obvious place so they will find it. Send them a text every once in a while. Tell them that you love them and that you believe in them. Text them, *"UR NEW! UR in CONTROL!"* Remind them of their triggers—both internal and external. Take action! Help them! You are in control! First, control yourself; then, you can offer a level of control for them.

Their internal triggers have to grow to see progress continuously. It's mental growth for both of you. Their accomplishments are your accomplishments when it comes to overcoming their issues. Their internal triggers need to be fed. Their ability to overcome situations is dependent on their growth. Like any activity that requires growth, there comes a time of stagnation. If both of you are practicing The RU NEW Principles every single day, there will never be stagnation. As you grow, you need to share your accomplishments with them. Talk about the situations you have overcome in the past and present. Be the example. Teach them your techniques for accomplishing a New State of Mind and Life. Do not allow the old-minded individuals of the world to be the influencing factor in their lives. You must continuously reinforce their abilities by promoting their internal triggers. Give them examples. Tell them what you are struggling with. By all means, tell them how you were able to conquer the issue. *The RU NEW Principles* are meant to be shared. Why not share them with the people that you love the most?

Lead by example. Live your life the way you want them to live theirs.

Start out as their guide. Live your life using The RU NEW Principles and teach by example. Have pep rallies! It sounds kind of crazy, doesn't it? But the energy of like minds is very powerful. It may be just a passing moment. Sitting at the kitchen table and asking each other if You Are New. Pick up the phone and give them a call. When they answer, holler on the phone, I Am New! Are You? Over a period of time, it will become an anticipated moment. It will develop excitement in both of you. Sounds crazy, doesn't it? But what do you have to lose? What you have been doing so far may not be working. Do you know that old saying that says if you want to make changes in your life, you must make changes in your life? How true that is. Something out of the ordinary is definitely impactful. That is what you're trying to accomplish. You're trying to make an impact. *The RU NEW Principles* will definitely make an impact in your life and theirs.

You may still get some resistance. They may still be lashing out or building a cocoon. There are moments when they do things that require discipline. The moment of discipline is a very critical moment for a young person that is dealing with various issues. If you are going to discipline your child, you must first discipline yourself. That means you must be disciplined. Lashing out blindly will only cause more damage. Prepare yourself for the moment ahead of time. Understand that you are always in need of growth. The most beneficial growth is becoming New. You must practice being New daily. By doing this, you become more understanding and tolerable. You will analyze a situation with an open mind. You will allow for their faults. Why? Because you understand where you came from and where you are going. The old you reacted a certain way. That way may not be conducive for your teenager's situation. But by reacting as a New Person, you will be far more effective. Use The RU NEW

RU NEW?

Principles before reacting. This will allow you to have faith, understanding, knowledge, and optimism. You must be tolerable but also firm. Being firm must first be rooted in the examples of your life. There is no rule book that tells you how to discipline your children. Yes, there are books that give you methods. The missing link in the few that I have read is that every child is unique; therefore, every situation is unique. You must understand who your child is and the issues that your child is having. You must grasp all of the aspects of their situation. This requires knowledge, tolerance, understanding, and the ability to put yourself in their situation. By raising them New, as long as you are practicing being New, your message of discipline will be far more effective. As your child grows in *The RU NEW Principles,* your need for discipline will become less likely. A New Child is a Child at Peace. If your child is at peace, your life will also be peaceful. Both of you are traveling in the same direction. You can now look at your family and feel confident that they can handle any situation that is put in front of them. They are at peace, and so are you. *ALL OF YOU ARE NEW!!*

You are now working together as one. You and your child are following the same path. Together you will be able to conquer the world. Everyone is confident and optimistic. All are tolerable and understanding. You are in control. Your child's self-esteem is growing along with a high level of confidence. They understand that they have support. They understand that you are setting the example by living *The RU NEW Principles.* Now you are walking the walk, and guess what? So Are They!

If you are not a single parent, naturally, there will be a significant other. They may not be living *The RU New Lifestyle,* but they should be. There may be a difference of opinion in parenting. This is a hurdle that you will have to overcome. The best way to overcome the situation is to allow your positive changes from being New to being influential in their transformation. It may take time for them to see the positive changes in your life. However, if you are truly practicing *The RU NEW Principles*, it is inevitable that they too will begin to understand the benefits of being New. Over time, they will see it and understand it. Seeing and knowing is all that it will take. Have patience.

Once your entire family is New, it will be time to build your inner circle. Positive energy is what your child needs in their life. Negative, miserable people are detrimental to your family's well-being. As your friends begin to see the changes in your family life, they will naturally become curious. This is an excellent opportunity to build your inner circle. Share *The RU NEW*

Principles with all your friends and family. If your child is surrounded by people that are practicing being New, they will grow tremendously faster. They will have a higher level of peace, which will be true for you as well. Keep in mind that everyone is unique. Some will resist more than others. Stay the course and be the example. Because you care for your child, you must do what is necessary to enhance their life. Surrounding them with positive energy is absolutely beneficial for both of you. Every aspect of their life will be moving in the right direction. A new direction. A New Life!

Develop your strategy. Learn who your child is. Take time to understand where they're going. Set Long-term and short-term goals. Be their mentor and their guide. Take an interest in their development. It will only help yours. Whatever condition they were in, they now are in control. They have a positive outlook. Sit down with them and share what your goals and ambitions are. Tell them how they can reach their goals faster by practicing *The RU NEW Principles.* This will create excitement and optimism. You are giving them reasons to better themselves; Reasons with results. The results are the positive changes in their life. You do not have to convince them that *The RU NEW Principles* work. They will see it for themselves. They will have confidence in themselves and their ability to conquer any situation. Now they are ready to pursue their goals and dreams. Now, your child can see the wonderful life in front of them. They are no longer living in yesterday. They are living today. They are New! Their Victory is Your Victory!

There is absolutely no reason why you should not encourage *The RU NEW Principles* for your children and your significant other. There are no negative aspects. You love your child, and you want the best for them. Do you want to give them every opportunity to succeed? Everyone in this world has obstacles to overcome. Most do not have the knowledge to overcome their situation. Your child is not that individual. They are living the life of being New. They see the world as their playground. They see opportunity and hope. They have the knowledge to handle any situation that may be thrown in front of them. They have their internal triggers, which allow them to have control. They have their external triggers and their support team. That support team is you, your family, and your inner circle. You now have a plan. The plan is *The RU NEW Principles*. No matter how bad or good the situation is, it can always get better. And it will, providing you have the tools to get there. The tools are *The RU NEW Principles!* Seeing the positive changes in your children and your family will be amazing! So every chance you get,

RU NEW?

ask them, *RU NEW?* Together, at the count of
three......

WE ARE NEW!!!!!

CHAPTER 11

STACK THE DECK

INNER CIRCLE

So here you are. You are definitely New. Your life has changed for the better. It does not matter where you were when you began this journey. Your family is on board as well. The benefits of *The RU NEW Principles* are completely evident now. Each day you are attaining another level. You're reaching a *Higher Level of New!*

You have noticed the difference in your relationships with coworkers and friends. They see the difference in you. It is completely apparent that your performance at work has increased. You can see the attitudes change around you. Your family is happy to see you so well-adjusted. So, how do you make larger increases in Newness? How do you compound your *Higher Levels of New?* Well, that is very simple. You expand your World of New. Create your *New Nation!* You build your inner circle. You are amazed at the benefits of being New. So why wouldn't you share this with your friends and family?

The first question to ask is, what level of New are you? At the beginning of your journey, you were able to convey the benefits of *The RU NEW Principles* by example. People will see the change in your attitude. A positive attitude. They will notice how you handle stressful situations and be curious. Your friends will be amazed at how well-adjusted you have become. How good your family life is? Your coworkers will see your increased production. They will be amazed by your attitude. Those that know you the best, your family, will be able to notice the positive changes in you and your life far better than anyone else. Oh, and as you continue practicing these principles, it will be more evident to those around you that there is something to *The RU NEW Principles.*

They will be curious and ask questions. You will be overjoyed to share. You have been sharing through your actions and reactions. They will ask what has changed. If you want them to reap the same rewards that you have attained, you want to share The RU NEW Principles. The New You is what you are sharing at the moment. They will want to learn about your secret. Tell them that you are reading this book and it has changed your life. Tell them about the positive impact on your family. Why edify and promote? One reason is that you will be helping a friend or a family member. There is no better feeling than knowing you positively impacted someone's life. You may be the difference in that person's situation. It may be somebody that they know. It may be their significant other, their child, or a family member. Sharing *The RU NEW Principles* has the potential to make a huge impact in someone else's life. That is one of the greatest rewards in life. Helping a brother or sister in need. There is a huge benefit in building your inner circle.

The benefits of surrounding yourself with New people are numerous. You know too well the feeling that comes over you when negative and pessimistic people surround you. It drags you down. It makes your life a struggle. It may cause stress and anxiety. I'm not saying to avoid those people. They may be in your family, or they may be a close friend. I am saying that if you are not willing to share these principles with them, you may be passing up the opportunity to turn their negative energy into positive. Would you rather put up with their little chicken attitude forever, or would you rather make a positive impact in their life and increase the positive energy around you? On the flip side, you definitely can recall when you were in the presence of an individual that is positive and optimistic. It brightened your day. It made you feel better. It gave you hope. Now that you are New, that person is you. Why not compound that feeling by surrounding yourself with people going in the same direction with a like attitude? If you do not share, they may never find out. I bet they will approach you with curiosity after a brief amount of time. Seize the opportunity to increase your inner circle. Change someone and change their life. You may be the difference when it comes to their child suffering from depression or anxiety. They may be suffering from addiction. Maybe social anxiety. There are a multitude of conditions where you will be able to make a difference.

Most people that you will run into are still living their old life. They are probably pessimistic and not very open-minded. They are those individuals that say, just because you say it's so doesn't make it so. We all have been around those individuals. You will usually get this type of response from a cousin or a friend. It is usually somebody that is comfortable with speaking their mind to you. And that's great! Why? It's because they know your past and are around you more than anyone else. Have you heard; that the proof is in the pudding? They will see the difference in your life. It may take a little time. Are they worth it? Of course, they are. Do you want to help them? Do you want to surround yourself with positive energy from people that are New? The proof is the changes in you. Is the proof in the pudding? Well, guess what, did you ever think you would be pudding? Yes, you are the pudding. The proof is in the pudding!

You will have casual first-time encounters with individuals in your daily life. Because they feel your positive energy, they will be comfortable with talking about personal subjects. I have seen it firsthand. The other day, a young man asked me if my attitude is always positive. I explained that I live my life by *The RU NEW Principles*. He immediately inquired. I explained that the principles apply to every aspect of your life. Through further conversation, he shared that his wife suffered from anxiety and periodic panic attacks. I shared the benefits of using internal and external triggers. Also, gave examples of external triggers and how to combat the onset of anxiety. I felt comfortable giving my contact info. Two days later, he sent me a text. He and his wife were excited. He said that in just two days of using the techniques, they had experienced positive results. This is an example of how *The RU NEW Principles* can positively impact someone's life. That is one of the greatest feelings that you can experience. To help someone in a time of need is what we should all be about. I am anxious to follow their progress. Just because of your energy, there will always be conversation opportunities. Never pass up an opportunity to make a difference in someone's life.

Your family will notice quicker than anyone. Normally, they are closer to you than anyone else. They can see the subtle changes. It will create curiosity. Over time, they will want to know what made the difference. They will encourage you to continue down your path even though they are not aware of the path you are traveling. They want to see you succeed and be happy. They will become extremely curious as they see the continued improvements in your life. Yes, the most critical people in our lives are normally our family. They usually have doubts. They usually have no problem telling you about their doubts. Even if they doubt the noticeable improvement will continue, they will normally be supportive. Your continued progress will be your opportunity to expound on *The RU NEW Principles*. You will have an opportunity to be a positive influence in their life. It will usually take longer with family to believe in the principles. Why? Because they've known you all of your life. They will judge you by your past. Today is a New Day. You must tell them that today is New and that You Are New! Tell them you are making changes in your life and would like to share your New found secret. In most cases, it is vitally important to have the support of your family. They are definitely a strong support group. Why would you want a negative support group? How can they be encouraging and negative at the same time? Outwardly, they are supportive. But internally they are pessimistic. That is why it is vitally important to share *The RU NEW Principles* with your family.

RU NEW?

They may be the most well-adjusted people that you know. Just as anything in life, it could be better. Aren't we all trying to get better? Better as a person? Better as a worker? Better as a friend or a family member? You will be a positive influence in their life, and you will be building your inner circle.

Your Friends. You may only have a few friends. Or you may be that individual that has countless friends. Regardless, your friends normally spend more time with you than anyone. They are normally a huge influence in your life. Your friends can be supportive and also critical. Your friends know you almost as well as your family does. Close friends are normally considered family anyway. You will probably be more comfortable sharing your newfound secret for a happier and more productive life with them. A true friend is overjoyed to hear about what you have found and what you are experiencing. They will be receptive to *The RU NEW Principles.* As a matter of fact, they will probably be the quickest to explore how *The RU NEW Principles* can benefit their life. Under normal circumstances, your closest friends are the biggest part of your day-to-day life. Why wouldn't you share these principles with them? The more time you take to share this with them, the less time you will reap the rewards of their newfound Positive Energy. More positive energy around you will only make you stronger. There may be situations in your friend's life that *The RU NEW Principles* may make the difference in whether or not their situation is resolved. Helping casual acquaintances is rewarding, but making a difference in your friend's life is absolutely phenomenal.

Coworkers and business associates are very beneficial to your inner circle. You spend at least 40 hours a week with these people. Maybe even more. They definitely have an impact on your attitude and energy. The most important goal of your job or business is financial gain. Performance and efficiency are two of the most important factors involved in advancements and increased monetary compensation. If you are surrounded by negative energy, it will affect your performance. Yes, You Are New, and you are practicing *The RU NEW Principles*. This alone will be extremely beneficial in your career or your business. By surrounding yourself with individuals that are moving in the same positive direction, you will multiply your success along with theirs. Increasing your inner circle at your job or business can do nothing but bring benefits: financial benefit and personal growth. You will reduce your anxiety and stress. You will look forward to going to work. Knowing that everyone in your work world is in your inner circle, you will be far more excited about showing up for work. You will be less likely to bring stress home. It's a win-win! Build your circle at work because it will take you to a *Higher Level of New.*

Building each other's positive energy results from building your inner circle. It is the power of numbers. If those around you are no longer stressed, your life is better. If they are supportive and encouraging, you have succeeded. Surrounding your family with like-minded people will build an environment for growth and contentment. Their growth is your growth. As they become New, you will attain a *Higher Level of New. The RU NEW Principles* will enhance every aspect of your life, and that will be compounded by building your inner circle.

This is not a club. It's a way of life! It's your life! You are in control! By being New, you can overcome every obstacle in your path. Everyone in your inner circle is your support team.

RU NEW?

Are they New? If the answer is yes, great! If the answer is no, then the reply is not yet. *RU NEW?* Yes! Are you ready for a *Higher Level of New?* Of course, *YOU ARE!*

Now get out there and live *The New Life!*

Show the world what *Being New* is all about!

CHAPTER 12

YOUR TOOL BOX TECHNIQUES

Now, there is no doubt in your mind. The *RU NEW Principles* will enhance your life like no other technique. This is a way of life. It's not a club. It's not a chat group. It's not a group of counseling sessions. *The RU NEW Principles* will be ingrained in you. It will be how you live your life. From the day that you begin, you will see the difference. I am speaking from personal experience. *The RU NEW Principles* will become your culture. You are knowledgeable. Now let's talk about Techniques. In this chapter, we will hone in on those techniques.

Let's start with *Internal Triggers*. First of all, let's identify what an internal trigger is. It is the weapon you use to combat the negative influences in your life. It's what you use when you feel the onset of stress and anxiety. It's what you say to yourself, internally or externally, that will trigger your response and defense. It is how you establish control.

There are many negative forces in our lives that pop up daily. It may be something that is said or it might be something that is done. It may be the negative energy that's being generated from an external source. But do not make the mistake; most of the negative thoughts are generated by you. That said, the only positive thoughts will also come from you. That is where an internal trigger plays its part. You feel the negative coming on. Yes, you may start to get anxious. Yesterday you would allow that to compound to the point where it would alter your attitude. For the most part, it would definitely alter that moment in time.

RU NEW?

You now have a weapon that allows you to cut those negative thoughts off at the pass. You look at yourself immediately and ask *RU NEW?* It may be a single question, or you may ask the question several times. Whatever you need to do to accomplish your goal, your goal is to gain control. And once you have established the question, now you are really ready to believe the answer. The answer is, "I Am New!" If you are like me, you will tell yourself often during the day, "I Am New!" There are moments when the feeling of negativity is so strong that it requires you to repeat it repeatedly until you establish control. That is the goal with an internal trigger. Once you have used your internal trigger many times with positive results, you'll understand the power of an internal trigger. Each moment you use your trigger, you are vaulting yourself into a *Higher Level of New*. The New You that is in control! If you are like most, you are in tune with your senses. By senses, it is meant that you respond well to touch, smell, and vision. External triggers rely on your senses. That is what makes them extremely powerful. Combining an external trigger with your internal will give you ultimate control.

What is an external trigger? The answer to that question is pretty much up to you. You are going to choose the object that will be your external trigger. It may be many things. It may be a sticky note on the bathroom mirror. Or it may be a figurine or a stuffed animal on your nightstand. It has to be something of significance. It needs to be something that triggers the question *RU NEW?* You begin establishing control of your day with the answer *I AM NEW!* The internal and external are working in conjunction.

As you journey out into the world, you must carry your external trigger. I highly recommend a medallion on a necklace or bracelet that you can put between your fingers and rub in a time of need. On that medallion is inscribed "*I AM NEW!*" The touch of that trigger in a time of need is crucial. You may use it from time to time. Or you may use it quite frequently. It depends on what you're dealing with. Put something in your pocket. I have a small bag with significant objects in it. One of them is a medallion that says *I AM NEW!* As I mentioned in the beginning, I have a pen that was a gift from my wife that says *I AM NEW*. If you are like most, you have a smartphone. An excellent external trigger can be utilized with reminders on your phone. You can set one a day that says *RU NEW/I AM NEW*. Depending on your situation, you may want to have several daily reminders. One set for the time that you arrive at work. I would recommend it when you arrive at the parking lot. But if you have a boss practicing *The RU NEW Principles*, they may not mind you looking at your phone during work hours to reach a *Higher Level of New.* It may be for the drive home. Maybe when you arrive home after work if your home is normally chaotic, it is up to you to decide the frequency of the reminders.

The internal and external triggers are your weapons—the weapons of ultimate control. As with any weapon, you must practice becoming masterful. This is a way of life. This is your life. You are in control. No matter what comes your way, you have the ability to see it, push back, and eliminate it. Build your knowledge of these principles, and you will gain strength. With strength comes control.

Anticipation. It is the art of identifying the onset. You know the signs and the feelings. You have experienced both in the past. It's not hard to get good at anticipating. In the past, more than likely, you attempted to ignore it. You tried to convince yourself that you were in control. Maybe, in some instances, you were. For some, ignoring the signs is only compounding the issues. Train yourself to anticipate. Think about what you are feeling when that trying situation attempts to consume you. I'm sure you already know how to identify the situation or the person. You need to practice getting proficient at identifying the onset in its early stages. Don't ignore it. Welcome it. You know it's coming. You know the feelings before they start to well up. You are prepared. You have identified the onset.

You have taken the first step in controlling whatever the issue is. You no longer ignore. You meet it head-on. You have the weapons to fight with. You have The RU NEW Principles! You put your internal and external triggers to work. Because you're developing the *I Am New*

RU NEW?

Mentality; you are getting good at anticipating and stopping it before it gets out of control.

There it is. You feel it. Before your heart begins to race or you get that nauseated feeling, you grab your external trigger. You activate your internal trigger and begin to meet the issue head-on. Touching or seeing your external trigger will automatically activate your internal trigger. Your internal will convince you that You Are New. It will convince you that you have control. You are controlling your mental state. Ultimately, you are changing your physical condition. Now you see how vital it is to anticipate the onset.

Control is the ultimate goal. Your first step is to control yourself. Only then will you be able to control your surroundings. You establish control by using your internal and external triggers. In the past, being the old you, you probably did not utilize triggers. Maybe you did. Utilizing the *RU*

New Triggers will definitely change the game. The principles are based on control. By getting proficient with control, you are now changing your life. No matter the situation or condition, the ultimate goal is to remain in control. It takes practice. You are striving for *Higher Levels of New*. The further that you travel down this path, the effort to gain control will become easier each moment. Once you have become proficient at control, you can apply your techniques to all aspects of your life.

Performance! Physical or mental. It may be at work or your business. It may be in the gym or around the house. It may be a task that requires mental exertion. Regardless of what it is, everything requires increased performance to acquire higher levels of accomplishment. There will always be a point of physical or mental exhaustion. The ability to push through first requires mental control. This is where your triggers become extremely beneficial. You are getting proficient at anticipation. Before you reach that moment of exhaustion, you are anticipating the onset. You begin programming your mind and body to push just a little bit more. You may or may not have the opportunity to use your external trigger. But you definitely have the ability to use your internal. Let's just take one example. A physical example. In our past, we have had the need to run for whatever reason. It may have been voluntary or involuntary. Both apply. Let's say you decided to run a certain distance somewhere in your life. You may have believed you could run a mile. But your body told you otherwise. There came that point of exhaustion. Your body was talking to you and your mind took over. You concentrated on the burning sensation and your inability to catch your breath. In the past, you may have given in to a lack of mental control and stopped. Now, with the addition of your internal and external triggers, you have the ability to push a little further. Your mind is a very powerful thing. It can either shut you down or keep you going. By utilizing your triggers, your mind will begin to convince your body that it is capable of one more step. You feel the burn. You trigger. Your mind begins telling your body that it is New. That you are in control. That you can overcome. You will be amazed at what you can do with this technique. You may not be running a marathon, but you are running your race. Yes, it takes conditioning of your body to create the ability to run that extra distance. But you must have control of your mind to get proficient at conditioning your body.

Physical and mental exertion applies to every aspect of your life. Staying at work that extra hour, writing that extra chapter when your eyes are trying to roll back in your head, cutting that

last acre of grass when the temperature is 95°
with 80% humidity, swimming that extra lap,
staying focused when someone is telling you a
story, You know where the needs are. You know
the roadblocks in your life. Everything requires
performance. Learning how to use your triggers
is vitally important. You may use your internal
or external trigger, or you may use both. You are
in control. That includes what method you use
to take that extra step. You have the tools and
the knowledge to push forward.

Knowledge opens so many doors. Knowledge is
strength, and strength is power. Power is control.
Knowledge of *The RU NEW Principles* is
beneficial in enhancing your life. Knowledge
comes with practice. Practice is up to you. By
using your triggers all through your day, you are
establishing the knowledge of their application.
Some situations are a no-brainer others not so
much. You may not realize that certain

situations have a negative effect on your life. But, by practicing *The RU NEW Principles* and using your triggers as often as you can, you will uncover unrealized aspects that have been minor hurdles. You are gaining knowledge. The changes will be subtle. Over time, you will understand that *The RU NEW Principles* have uncovered avenues for improvement. It may be something that has been affecting you mentally or physically. You just didn't realize that it was the root cause of your mental and physical fatigue. As you reach *Higher Levels of New,* you will experience higher levels of energy and less fatigue. You are establishing control of your mental and physical condition.

Your mental state of mind definitely influences your physical condition. As previously discussed, your ability to handle a physical condition is strongly influenced by your mental state. Who has control of your mental state of mind? Of course, you do. By utilizing your triggers when you are experiencing health issues, you will have the ability to cope at a higher level. Your mind has a tremendous amount of control over your physical condition. Using your triggers and establishing mental control will help you through your condition. Your mental state of mind can be a contributing factor to a speedier recovery.

I AM NEW! I am in control! I can beat this! I will not allow this illness to consume me! You are creating positive energy. A defeatist attitude creates negative energy. Negative energy creates doubt and despair. Positive energy is created by being New. Use your triggers. Create positive energy. Take control of your mental state and it will positively affect your physical condition.

Having control of your life's mental and physical aspects will establish tolerance—the tolerance for any situation or the tolerance of others. Being tolerable comes with time. People just have the knack for getting under your skin. Remind yourself that You Are New, internally and externally, before you step into the realm of negativity, before you arrive at work, walk into a family gathering, rr any stressful situations. The RU NEW Principles will give you the ability to tolerate their negative nonsense. You are ahead of the game because UR NEW, and you are in control. Some situations may take more effort than other; Anticipation, Triggers, and Control. Negative is no match for you. If you really want to blow their mind, walk in with a shirt that says "I Am New"! They will have that calf looking at a new gate look. They will be looking at a Totally New Person!

Getting yourself under control, regrouping, and identifying yourself. Identifying yourself as a New You! Use the techniques. *The RU NEW*

RU NEW?

Principles. You now have the tools to conquer the world!

YOU ARE NEW!!!

CLOSING THOUGHTS

The RU NEW Principles are a passion! Due to a necessity for a life change, I began exploring methods to gain control of my life. A comment was made many years ago during a meeting I was attending. During the meeting, someone made a statement that implied a new attitude. The word New stuck with me that day. Due to the fact that I can be extremely analytical, I began pondering the word New. In my thought processes, I realized that the concept of New applied to every aspect of everyone's life. It's a commonly used word. I doubt that many people have studied the concept in depth. And I began to understand that the word New was an extremely powerful concept. A whole set of principles could be derived from the concept. At the time, my life was relatively uneventful. Yes, there were moments of stress, but nothing extremely significant. Then, several years ago, there was a life-changing event. A medical emergency that nearly took my life. Or so I thought. It was later found to have been caused by stress. Yes, I had a severe panic attack due to an undiagnosed ailment. In the previous chapter on health, I shared the particulars. Once I was released from the hospital, I knew that I had to make some changes in my life. I began pondering and experimenting. Then suddenly, the concept of being New hit me like a ton of bricks. I began intensely studying the concept of being New. I applied it to my life with tremendous results. Once I realized the power of *The RU NEW Principles,* I began applying them to every aspect of my life.

The changes in my life were tremendous and very evident. Evident to the point that people became curious. Many comments were made about the positive changes in my life. There were people in my life that were aware I had the ability to write. With curiosity and knowledge, they encouraged me to put this concept into a book. Call it procrastination, if you will. I was not sure how I wanted to relay the message. I wanted the book to be extremely beneficial to anyone who read it. I was living my life experiencing Higher Levels of New every day. I began to realize that there will always be a benefit from practicing *The RU NEW Principles.*

Some of you may be exactly as I am. I do not have the ability to read quickly. Therefore, reading was a challenge for me. Reading slow translated into writing slow. It took me quite a while to realize that pen and paper were not conducive to my abilities. It hit me one day like a sledgehammer. In a previous employment situation, I was required to create daily reports. There was a system in place. It was a dictation system. There it was! I would utilize a dictation program to write my book. Here we are, in the present time, where I am dictating these life-changing principles into book form. And how life-changing they are!

Along my journey, I've had people brought into my life for a reason. That reason, on many occasions, was to share *The RU NEW Principles.* I have spoken to people with relationship problems. Some with Addiction and others with anxiety. Some with severe anxiety that resulted in panic attacks. In all cases where I was given the opportunity to share at length, *The RU NEW Principles* have had 100% positive feedback.

The casual encounters have been phenomenal as well. When appropriate, I have shared the general concept of being New. In the work environment, I have periodically asked, Are You New? Those who heard me ask the Question in the past immediately raised their hand. For those that hadn't, pride kicks in or a lack of knowledge of the concept, and they refuse to raise their hand. It isn't until I explain the concept of Being New, will they raise their hand. From that point forward, they will always raise their hand when asked if They Are New.

The RU NEW Principles are extremely powerful! They should be shared whenever the opportunity arises. As previously said, this is not a club. It's a way of life. It's a way to live your entire life. It will benefit you and everyone around you. Study it and apply it. You definitely, will not regret it.

The application of *The RU NEW Principles* will make a positive impact on all aspects of your life. There is not a single part of your life that these principles will not positively affect you. You may have a life of happiness, joy, and prosperity. But, there is still a need in your life to make things better. We should always strive to better ourselves and those around us. Then there are others who are in moments of extreme need. These principles can and will help them through their moment of need. If you have a condition that requires professional help, such as doctors or counselors, you must continue seeking their advice and treatment. As said, they cannot be with you 24 hours a day. Your struggles are real and normally are strongest during moments of solitude. This is where *The RU NEW Principles* will help you overcome your situation.

Your mental abilities strongly influence your physical issues and limitations. These principles will strengthen your mind and, thus, strengthen your body. Increased performance converts into better health. Wow, what a concept! Allow yourself time to grow. Time to Become New!

"If you want to make changes in your life, you have to make changes in your life. "

RU NEW?

"If you want to be New, you must practice being New!"

"With knowledge comes strength. With strength comes power. With power, you establish control. "

"Saying that it is so does not make it so. The proof is in your actions. "

"Do not judge me by my past. You will miss out on The New Me if you judge me by my past. At this moment, all you have to judge me by is my present. As you begin to realize that I am A New Person and this is a New Day, you will understand that the past does not dictate my future. My future is based on the simple question of Am I New? What you should judge me by is the changes in me today with the allowance for growth."

RU NEW?

"Striving for wisdom doesn't have to wait on age. Wisdom is better found within the transformation into the New You."

"Anxiety is a product of physical existence. Your uncontrollable mental path is the culprit. You must regain control one question at a time. Your Newness will diminish the frequency and intensity of each episode."

"Increased performance is only attained with mental growth. "

"Mental growth is the product of practicing self-control."

"If you want it, Go Get It!"

"You say you want a better life. Then do something about it."

"Tools and weapons are useless unless you use them!"

RU NEW?

You now have the tools. You have a powerful weapon to fight back against the negative situations in your life. You have the ability to make your life better. You must practice *The RU NEW Principles* daily. It may require asking the question quite frequently during the day. The more you practice the Principles, the Newer you will get. You may feel that you are strong enough and you are content with your life as it is. But I can guarantee there are people in your life that would benefit tremendously from reading this book and applying *The RU NEW Principles* to their lives. I feel that it is my duty to share the principles with anyone who is receptive or in need. And that is pretty much everyone in my life or is briefly passing through. I hope, for their sake that is true for you as well. Sharing is Caring!

Soon to come, there will be a sequel. It will be titled *A Higher Level of New!* The exact date of

RU NEW?

creation is not known at the moment. It will be in the near future. It will expound on the techniques shared in this book. It will vault you even further into this *Wonderful World of Being New!*

The beginning is the end! And the end is the beginning! So I leave you with these questions!

Are You New?

Are you in control?

Do you want a better life?

Do you want to improve every aspect of your life?

Do you want to be a better person?

Do you want to improve your quality of life?

RU NEW?

Do you want improved performance?

Do you want that raise and promotion?

Do you want to improve your profit margin?

Do you want to be more successful?

Do you want to eliminate anxiety?

Do you want to make your anxiety a thing of the past?

Do you want to establish control over your Addiction?

Do you want a happy and prosperous life filled with joy and contentment?

Then I ask you the final and most important question

RU NEW?

If your answer is "not yet," then your reply should be "*I WILL BE!*"

RU NEW?

Just the fact that you're making steps in a positive direction to become New, the final answer is

I AM NEW!

ACKNOWLEDGEMENT

My family is my inspiration. They are my support. The encouragement and inspiration are priceless. They have witnessed my transformation and given such wonderful acknowledgment. I will be forever grateful for their support.

Lois, my wife, has been a tremendous asset in the development of this book. Her thoughts and ideas have been tremendously beneficial. Her contribution is priceless. She is my biggest supporter!

Thank you, Pop, for being the example of the man I want and should be. Your support and guidance have been amazing. Thank you!

My children and grandchildren have been inspirational. They have been an incredible example of what life is truly about. I have been blessed. I have watched their day-to-day life and the struggles they have gone through. They have conquered all of their life struggles and emerged victorious with an attitude of being *NEW!*

I would like to give thanks for the diversity in my life. Diversity has been very instrumental in the development of *The RU NEW Principles.* I am extremely fortunate to have been exposed to negative people. They have been beneficial in my transformation. Without the negative situations and people, the inspiration may have been nonexistent. Therefore, I would like to acknowledge the benefits of being exposed to the negative of this world. It has allowed me to become *NEW!* It has been the driving force in the development of *The RU NEW Principles.*

You have been enlightened! You now have the tools to conquer anything that life throws at you!

RU NEW?

You are on the path to Enrichment!

You are New!!!

Soon to come, you will be able to launch your life to another level with:

"A Higher Level of New!"

www.RUNEW.org